Cameos

WOMEN FASHIONED BY GOD

Helen W. Kooiman, a housewife·
and mother of four living in
Fullerton, California, has written
three other books for women:
"Please Pray for the Cabbages"—
entrancing and spiritually illuminating
experiences with children—
"Joyfully Expectant"—inspiring
meditations for mothers-to-be—
and "Small Talk"—a collection
of heartwarming family experiences
that first appeared in "Christian
Times."

Cameos

Women Fashioned by God

HELEN W. KOOIMAN

Tyndale House Publishers
Wheaton, Illinois

Coverdale House Publishers, Ltd.
London, England

Library of Congress Catalog Card Number 68-56393

ISBN 8423-0200-X, Cloth
ISBN 8423-0201-8, Paper

Copyright © 1968 Tyndale House Publishers
Wheaton, Illinois

Eleventh Printing, March 1973
117,000 copies in print

Printed in U.S.A.

Dearest Mother

I hadn't told you because I wanted to surprise you, but this book is dedicated to you, Mother. I know readers will understand when I say that to me, you are the dearest Cameo of all. Oh, I know you would have laughed and objected, reminding me you had never attained any greatness. But that's just it—because you were so very ordinary you were extraordinary! In a way, you represent the *many* very ordinary women who have always made up the greater share of the world.

You spent your life scrubbing floors, ironing, washing walls, and sewing. These tasks, and all the other laborious, unglamorous, back-breaking, menial jobs were yours. And you didn't complain! You knew heartache—when Daddy died and you were left with two small children to support and me on the way; no one else knew about me until my existence became obvious. You were a widow for over forty years, and because Daddy's illness had taken all our money, you had to go to work to support the four of us. You trudged through snowbanks and walked long blocks from one job to the other in the heat of Iowa summers. Oh, Mother, you were a choice Cameo!

How faithful you were in training us in the way we should

go, guiding us to our Heavenly Father and his Son. Now, as I think of you, I know you are one of his "Living Gems," at rest, complete in Christ. Heaven seems even more desirable as I look toward that day when I can join you there.

And now it's finished—this book—the undertaking which you were so pleased about and for which you prayed. When you were no longer here to pray, Mother, how I missed the feeling that you were praying for me, and no longer could I get on the phone to talk things over with you. You were so much more than a mother—you were a friend and confidant, as well.

So, one morning in a moment of desperate need for intercessory prayer, I phoned Donna. That began a pattern, and every morning as I approached my desk to work on the book I dialed her number. Donna, in her exuberant way, would say, "Helen! Whose story are you doing today?" and I would tell her. She would get on the phone and call others. This book was covered with prayer. I felt like I was almost on "holy ground" as I wrote it, and it was a thrilling experience. God helped me, and only a few know the personal battles that were fought and the victories won! If the hearts of readers are blessed and their lives helped as much as mine has been in the compilation of this, then we will know even more fully that our prayers have been answered. Yes, Mother, your prayers, too!

At a time of sorrow when I most needed the strength and help others can give, these stories of other women's experiences spoke to my heart. How good God is! Of course he knew all along.

And then the letters started arriving from the women subjects. Always, it seemed, right at the very moment when I needed a special bit of help, a word of encouragement, I'd walk to the mailbox and there would be a letter from Marianna Slocum who has experienced such heartache, or one from Joyce Landorf who not too long ago had laid her mother to rest. Then the one from Dale Evans Rogers reminding me, "What a treasure you have waiting in heaven for you...." And Lila Trotman wrote, saying, "Isn't it thrilling knowing the One who never ever makes a mistake, your darling mother is at home...", and letters from many others. I could only thank God for the reality of Christ and the assurance I had that you were with him, and for these dear ones who took the time to send those words of understanding.

I wouldn't want anyone reading this book to think: "Oh, I could never attain what those women have attained!" No, the women here would be the first to say they themselves have not attained, that it is God who has accomplished anything worthwhile in their lives.

How wonderful that God, in his goodness, gives all kinds of experiences to all kinds of women, and we can learn and be helped by what God has done in others! And that's the purpose of this book—to show God's hand at work fashioning the lives of some of his children. The chipping, carving, and sculpting are all necessary by a craftsman if the gem is to emerge a thing of beauty. Thus it was, as editing on these stories progressed, I began to think of these women as precious jewels, "Cameos" being fashioned by the Master Craftsman. I know each woman whose story is presented would echo what you, Mother would have said, "Not unto us, O Lord, not unto us, but unto thy name give glory, for thy mercy, and for thy truth's sake" (Psalm 115:1).

Your loving daughter,

Helen

My Thanks . . .

I am deeply grateful to the women who so graciously responded, took the time and made the effort to provide information which gave the insights needed in order to write their stories.

Then, I am indebted beyond measure to these organizations and people: To Dr. Benjamin Elson, Executive Director of Wycliffe Bible Translators, Inc., for making available to me their Tzeltal file, the film *God Speaks Tzeltal Now,* and for his invaluable help and suggestions in the Marianna Slocum story; to Mary Ann Mooney (daughter of the late William Nyman, first Secretary-Treasurer of Wycliffe) who suggested Marianna's story and spent time with me in the obtaining of it; and to Cornell Capa, Magnum Photos, Inc., *Life* magazine photographer who provided the picture of Marianna taken among the Tzeltal Indians. To Mr. Frank Pickell of the Fred Dienert Advertising Company, who carefully checked the Millie Dienert story; and to the Southwest Baptist Conference women meeting at Forest Home for allowing me to attend their Spring 1967 Retreat in order to interview Mrs. Dienert. To Art Rush, Manager for Dale Evans Rogers, for reading the manuscript and supplying information; and the Fleming H. Revell Co. for permission to quote from Dale's books; also I wish to acknowledge the help received from reading Elise Miller Davis' book *The Answer Is God,* published by McGraw-Hill, for valuable background information it provided. To Keith Miller, author of the best-selling book *Taste of New Wine* and *The Second Touch,* for his suggestions and recommendations out of which we chose to use Olivia Plummer's story. To Betty Greene, Addie Rosenbaum, Joyce Enright, Lorne and Lucy Sanny for their contributions to the Lila Trotman story, and The Navigators for permission to quote from the booklets *Born to Reproduce, Great Is Thy Faithfulness, The Glen Eyrie Story,* and *Dawson Trotman the Pathfinder.* To Jane Dickenson for her gentle reminder and assistance in the Marj Saint Van Der Puy story, and to Missionary Aviation Fellowship for going into their files to supply letters and information. Also to the officers and personnel at MAF for their interest and willingness to share some of their history in the Betty Truxton story. To Dr. and Mrs. Marchant King for their gracious hospitality and facts supplied to tell the story of their daughter, Dr. Ruth Dix; and to Dr. Ralph Byron for suggesting the story be told; and to my dear friend Marjorie Chartrand (who was born on the mission field where Dr. Dix is serving, and went to school with Richard Dix) for assistance in the telling of this story. To Campus Crusade for Christ for letting the background story of their organization be told.

To all of you—and the many I cannot mention individually— may God bless your hearts through the reading of this book; there are no words to adequately express my gratitude.

What An Opportunity!

As you read the life-stories of these fifteen women, I wonder if you realize what an unprecedented opportunity is being given to you?

First, there is the opportunity of being introduced in a very personal way as you become acquainted with some of the inner working of God in each woman's life.

Then, where else could you meet these wonderful women? Many are wives of well-known men in today's Christian world. Where would you—or they—have the time or the occasion to sit down for such an intimate conversation!

The author, Helen Kooiman, has given us small glimpses into their lives, yet enough for us to know that everyone has a Valley of Shadows. Their courage and faith will inspire you, for pain and conflict is part of being human, and this is where Jesus Christ meets us.

I once thought it was up to me to arrange the experiences of life and the theology I knew into an artistic design. God does not ask us to make neat little patterns so that everything fits together. Through Evelyn Underhill, I found this truth again (*Mount of Purification*, p. 27. Longman's, London 1960):

"All he asks us to do is to weave up all he gives us, however odd it looks, into the fabric of our lives . . . not to puff us up . . . but to bring us nearer to what he wants and intends. Often his great works are done through those who are in the dark themselves."

Rosalind Rinker

Contents

Cameo one

Death of an "All-American Wife"

Olivia Plummer

"When God's Son died he sent an earthquake and an eclipse—when Olivia Plummer died to self God sent Gert Behanna and Keith Miller—same thing!" So says Olivia Plummer of the two people God used to shake her up and end her years of searching.

Keith Miller, author of the best-selling *Taste of New Wine**, describes this shaken vessel of humanity in his book as a vivacious party-girl who did the twist and told shocking stories to mixed groups. Dark blonde, blue eyes, attractive, the type of woman men turn to look at a second time. The type, too, that other women wish their male companion hadn't seen!

But that was in the "before" days. Still vivacious and attractive, Olivia Plummer now has a Christ-controlled personality. She describes herself as "a compulsive person by nature, given more to hostilities than gentleness, quick tempered, sharp tongued." But she gained a new nature, an attractive one, as she describes in her own words.

* * * * *

*Published by Word Books, Waco, Texas

I was born in Laredo, Texas, in 1934 to very handsome, upper-middle-class parents. As an only child I was idolized by my father and life was normal until my tenth year. Then a horrible accident resulted in my mother receiving burns over sixty percent of her body. She lay in an upstairs bedroom for a year, intermittently screaming to die when not heavily sedated by drugs. My father, unable to bear the sound and the stench, traveled extensively. My mother recovered, divorced my father, and she and I moved to San Antonio to live with my adored grandfather. Tragedy was to stalk our family, for within the year my father drank himself to death, granddaddy died and I acquired a stepfather.

That once-idolized child of that lovely couple, who lived in a nice home and had just everything, became a fat, loud-mouthed, attention-seeking pre-teenager. Throughout these years my family were church-centered in name. I attended Sunday school by hoofing it on my own. I don't know why actually, but as I look back now, I think "The Hound of Heaven" must surely have been in pursuit.

My teenage years were the most unproductive time of my life. My mother was a full-fledged alcoholic then. She followed Daddy in death by ten years—both were drunkards at forty-two years of age.

I graduated from high school at sixteen with poor grades and a poor attitude. A big bluff, I went off to a still lonelier place, the University of Texas. I lived for parties and good-looking dates. I did manage to rack up a few honors—Blue Bonnet Bell nominee ("sweetheart of school" was chosen from these), a Delta Zeta sorority pledge award, a plaque honoring me for the greatest grade-point increase from the previous semester and sweetheart of Delta Sigma Phi social fraternity. My future husband belonged to this fraternity. I was always bewildered at Al's lack of possessiveness. When his fraternity brothers would dance and fuss over me, the dream girl, he swelled with pride instead of bristling at their attention. Possessiveness has ever been a part of my nature because of my lack of security in relationships with others. But here was someone who showed me real freedom and love. Al Plummer had a winning smile and genial laughter, and in my bids to be the life of the party, he always played the straight man for me.

When I married Al it was not for love—until I met the living Lord I didn't know what love was! I married a man who said he felt I was God's gift to him. For someone who had been nothing but a nuisance since ten years of age, this was a revelation! We married in the Episcopal Church, attended by my curiously sober mother; I was eighteen years old then and a junior in college.

My marriage was anything but a success. In later years my laughing, carefree husband was to become a compulsive gambler, frequently losing all his paycheck and away from home every night of the week. God was a swear word, not a comfort, not a Person. I remember going to church during those times and thinking, "Where is that peace they talk about?"

Outwardly we personified the "All-American" couple—three beautiful children, well known socially, active workers in our church, and prosperous in business. No one knew the hell inside. I went to church on Sunday and dutifully prayed, but no lights turned on within and my circumstances didn't change. I escaped my problems by becoming involved in other people's lives. What had at first been a desire to block out my own hell by living the joys and sorrows of others ended up being a very dark place full of resentments, jealousies and vicious gossiping.

If I tend to overemphasize the ugliness in my life, it is to show that God can really make a silk purse out of just any old thing, to quote my "adopted mother," Gert Behanna. There was utter poverty in my spiritual life. My emotional stability hung by the barest of threads. Of course, I was now on tranquilizers. I lived for nothing, loved nothing and nobody, and dreamed constantly of death.

We had been married three years when Junie Marie was born. We loved her dearly. Dutifully baptized at four months, our blue-eyed, pink-cheeked infant smiled and cooed while a host of god-parents and relatives looked on. Al worked in the funeral business with his father, and time off for family outings was rare. One day when Junie was about seven, her brother five and baby sister three, Father was coerced into a family picnic.

It was a cloudy day, the sky had an ominous look about it and there was a hint of fall in the air. It was the kind of day when you make one last try to hold on to summer and its warmth. After many trips loading the car (were we really going for only a couple of hours?), we all climbed in and Al and I gritted our teeth. I looked at him and mumbled, "This family-togetherness is fun, isn't it?"

Then the skies opened and rain began to come down, gently at first compared to the tears falling down our children's cheeks. "Don't worry, Mommy, I'll ask God to stop the rain for our picnic," said Junie. She did. God did! And we had our picnic. Today, whenever I hesitate to pray for something or someone, I remember that day and our little girl who dared in her innocence to approach Almighty God about the weather. Our children have since taught us much about prayer and God!

Two years after our first child was born came Billy, a red-faced, angry baby who cried for the first two years of his life. I hated him! There were times I actually wanted to pick him up by the feet and bash his head against the wall. Nauseated with horror at my thoughts, I somehow stumbled through the days.

Al and I had little communication, and I felt he didn't love or care about me and the children. Somehow I had the strength to keep the family together amid mountains of bills and hours of loneliness.

Physical ailments are dandy release mechanisms. I spent hours in the doctor's office, thankful that—even though I paid him—here was someone who listened and in some way cared about my welfare. Dr. Dan Bacon, a personal friend and family physician, once said in an effort to give me some kind of hope, "You know, Olivia, you could land an airplane if you had to!" Big deal, I thought, what I wanted was a strong man to carry my burdens, not me to be a psuedo-man!

Al's own particular brand of hell is his story to tell. But let me say that today neither of us regrets those years. Every past experience and problem has served to advance the gospel. I swell with pride and love when I hear my husband tell some person: "Yes, I know what it is like to be a failure, to be afraid to be a real man. I know what it feels like to hate your parents and wife. I escaped to gambling; what's your escape, friend? Let me tell you how I gave my life to a Business Manager who straightened out all my problems—his services are free and guaranteed to work."

But I also have to confess that Al Plummer doesn't look good to me without Jesus Christ. Lest this sounds harsh—nothing looks good to me without Jesus Christ!

Our social life today may seem very dull to some, compared to what it once was. Jesus doesn't belong in the forced gaiety atmosphere which once absorbed our time and attention. Our days of charity organizational work are over, too, which once claimed endless hours, days, weeks. Our own particular brand of Jesus, we have come to see, is needed to work quietly among neighbors, friends and businessmen, and we have found true satisfaction and contentment with our new social life.

Because Al was on the church vestry and was Sunday school superintendent, and I was involved in the usual women's church activities, we were invited to Camp Capers, an Episcopal Church camp, for small-group dynamic leadership training sessions. Here we were thrown in among real Christians and began to hunger for that special something they had. I can't describe what it was, except that these people had real joy, not forced gaiety, and a direction in their lives. Most of all, love radiated from them. That was in the summer of 1959, and we have still maintained true friendships from those training sessions. With God as a bridge, time and distance have no meaning.

At one of those training camps I volunteered to sit on a panel group along with a highly educated clergyman, a Bible expert and a Christian education director. I had never even opened the Bible before, and here I was, a panel member supposedly qualified to answer questions from the audience composed of bishops, priests, lawyers, doctors and professors and dedicated lay people. I was so frightened; my whole life was a sham and a sinking feeling assured me it wouldn't be long before the audience knew it, too! I prayed at that moment my first really sincere prayer, "God, if you will be with me, I promise I won't be scared."

For a long time afterward, my prayers were to follow that pattern: "God, if you will do this for me, I will do so and so for you . . ." Since then I have learned beyond a doubt that what Paul said in Ephesians 2:8-9 is really true: "For by grace you have beeen saved through faith; and this is not your own doing, it is the gift of God—not because of works, lest any man should boast."

After that silent prayer on the panel the discussion began. I can only say God spoke through me; he answered questions submitted to me with a wisdom I do not possess. God performs miracles hourly, right around us that we don't comprehend.

In effect I began to die that day and was able to see the real me in the light of the living Lord. What I saw wasn't the ugliness of my marriage, not the failure of the church to help me, not the lousy friends I had nor the rotten deal I felt life had dealt me—what I saw was my sin, unjustified, unreconcilable. *I was the sinner, not the victim of sinners.*

Ever the first step, yet the hardest to take, is to admit you are a sinner. I see people all the time who don't want to be healed and changed, even though their life is a living hell; they would rather whine and complain. Whoever it was who said, "Lord, change the world starting with me," knew the simple secret of dynamic Christian living.

I left that camp session shaken to the core, knowing that something very profound had happened to me, but not entirely comprehending. God's Holy Spirit was working in my heart, though I did not understand then.

About this time I discovered I was pregnant with our third child and I prayed my second sincere prayer: "God, please let me miscarry." Our marriage was too shaky, it seemed to me, to stand this. I contracted a series of virus infections, all before the third month, which could have caused defects as does German measles. With German measles at such a time the chances for a defective fetus are fifteen percent; our odds for an abnormal baby were seventy-five percent. Months of doubt ate into what sanity I had left, and at seven months of pregnancy I took a large overdose of tranquilizers; I had reached rock bottom. I took enough of the tranquilizers to literally stun a horse but outside of minor grogginess I was not fazed by the medicine.

Several years later I was at a Saturday night school carnival, surrounded by noisy masses of parents and children who were positively deafening. I stood at the dart board, frantically trying to keep children out of the way of haphazardly thrown darts.

My head aching and my feet sore, I vowed I'd never volunteer to help out again. Then through the maze of meandering people popped a smiling, precious face, dominated by large, black eyes and long, black eyelashes—a real beauty, people said. Clutched in her dainty hands was a forty-cent pepper plant, paid for out of a fifty-cent weekly allowance. This was Christina's way of telling me how proud she was to have her mother work at her class concession. This was the baby I couldn't bear to have born! Today she is a monument to God's kindness and grace.

But soon after my failure at suicide something happened that everyone dreams about. A relative died and left me thousands of dollars. I thought happily, we could make a new start. But since lack of money was only a symptom of the problem, the new beginning fizzled fast.

I now had money to support the children and myself. Al had been a drag too long, and I moved him out. For years I had screamed divorce. I meant it now! But Al and I were more miserable apart than together. Poor, lonely humans, we consider being hated better than not being thought of at all! So with persistance as one virtue we again made a stab at the happy institution of holy wedlock.

When I first saw Keith Miller, I knew he had found what I had been searching for. Using some of Keith's own jargon, I got him aside and "puked my life story all over him." Keith never flinched. He told me that he had done many of the same things I had done. "I know exactly how you feel!" he said. "Next week I am starting a prayer group that will be full of people with problems just like yours."

Could there really be other people like me? No, surely not! At least, they weren't in the church; everyone there was smiling. They were all happy people, why, their very countenance showed this! No, I was the only lost soul in our church . . . or was I? I was soon to find out.

That Thursday night was to initiate four years of Thursday night prayer groups. My rebirth began in a small group of "strugglers" and even at the time of this writing (six years later), I need to follow the basic steps laid out in those early meetings to stay alive spiritually.

The discipline established was a daily quiet time composed of prayer, Bible reading and listening to prayers. I still require Christian fellowship found in similar groups, nourished by the sacraments of the church, and the need to accept the fact that I am a sinner, and only through giving my will to God *daily,* committing my life to him *daily,* does my life have direction and purpose.

For some, a life of walking in the Spirit is like a fast-moving river, rippling and twisting along its way, unable to stop or control its actions; for others, a life committed to God is like a peaceful, calm lake. It's been my experience that the still-lake type yearns to be the bounding river, and vice-versa. But it really doesn't matter; it's God who plans what type of witness you shall be. Your job is to be willing to endure the scraping along the river bottom to get rid of the debris, rocks and sunken tree stumps.

I wish that I could say my life changed overnight; it changed radically but painfully slow. Like Lazarus, when Jesus called him forth from the tomb, I was still bound in the burial strips, and some of the strips have taken years to unwind.

Al came to our second group meeting, defensive and critical. Gert Behanna was the speaker that night. Gert, in her sometimes brusque way, offended Al, to put it mildly. Al swore and fumed about her all week long. He spent hours planning the perfect rebuttal, and went a second time to hack away "at that big shot somebody who thinks she can just say anything to anybody!" But there was no Gert at the meeting. What a letdown for him!

"All right," he said, "I can wait—I'll get her next week!" But by the next week, Al was caught—hook, line and sinker. He committed his life to Jesus Christ and set about the business of putting his own house in order. When this story was related to Gert Behanna, she beamed and said, "Isn't it marvelous what God can do with our mistakes!" Isn't it, indeed! God has done more with my mistakes than ever with my good intentions.

Life became a fast-moving river for us, and every milestone was a blessing. In Christ we had a marriage. In Christ we were a family. We still had our arguments, what couple doesn't—but Al and I found our reaction time shorter. Whereas we once used to go for days without speaking, we found now that after a few hours of pouting we could kiss and make up.

Al began being more courteous and respectful. Nothing convinces a wife of eight years that her husband has changed as does gentlemanly courteousness. I tried to be less dominating and nagging. "Dear Christ, let me love and accept this man just like he is," I found myself praying. And, you know, either Al began to change or I began to accept him—but I suspect that something very special was happening to both of us.

When the mainspring of a watch is pulled out, all the springs pop out. The "mainspring" that had held me together for so many years was tension and pressure—when this was removed my parts popped out all over the place. When roused to anger I have been known to put sailors to shame. God began to convict me of these faults. He wanted me to assume the rightful role of being a gentlewoman, subject to her husband's desires, and in all manner loving and kind. That was a large order for me and still is, but some days, when I have made it, a feeling of peace fills me and I know that the swallowed pride, or ugly thoughts not spoken were worth all the price I had to pay. Then there are days when I seem to go one step forward and two steps back. Perhaps one of the marks of a Christian is that he is continually able to pick himself up after falling down.

We had reached a pinnacle, and Al and I went joyously forth witnessing to groups as to how Christ had changed our lives. One day we prayed that if it were God's will we would go anywhere—even to the ends of the earth. Peter Marshall said, "Watch what you pray for; you may get it." In one month's time we moved to Victoria, Texas, lock, stock and barrel. Al and I never took prayer casually from that time on. Though difficult to break family ties and leave friends whom we had known for ten years, we sallied forth, prepared to conquer Victoria in the Lord's name.

We purchased a motel, mortgaging everything we owned except our clothes, and while my husband set about learning the business I awaited the birth of our fourth child. The church was soon like home to us and we plunged into church work. Then, as convicts, drunks, lonely salesmen and loose women came into the motel we began to minister to them. We truly entered a world that we never knew existed. But as some stories must

have a sad ending, so did this one. One year later we were
bankrupt. Oh, the many lessons we have learned in the years
since!

We have come to see that one can be a failure in man's eyes
and yet a success to God's. We realized that we had been
holding onto "religion" but denying the power thereof. And we
have come to see that one never quite has the courage of his
convictions until he has tested them and discovered that God
says what he means. "I am with thee always, even until the ends
of the earth" is very meaningful in our experience.

God has continually blessed us with understanding friends
who, through these past few years, have prayed for us
constantly, cried with us frequently, and offered financial
assistance, too. Every morning at 6:30 we assemble for family
devotions. How thankful we are for the relationship we have
with our four children. Al and I know that Jesus Christ is in
that room with us, and as we thank him for all his blessings we
are supremely happy and thankful for what he has done in
saving each of us. Through Christ I am a new creation; I've
been freed from my past. Without him I can do nothing—I
would strangle to death on my past; with him I have life and
breath and depth and love.

Cameo two

Woman With A Past-- And a Future

Regina Ramsay

When Regina Ramsay stands to speak to a group of delinquents at a prison, training school, juvenile hall, or some other place of correction, a flood of memories sweeps over her. Pleasant thoughts and memories they are not! As she sees bitterness etched clearly on the hardened faces, her own unfortunate past—the awful years of her youth—rushes before her like a fast-playing film. She longs to reach out and embrace these people, to release them from the hurt, humiliation and anguish she knows they are experiencing—and which she experienced for twenty-eight years.

"I'm not a speaker," she says. "I'm more like the demoniac we read about in the Bible who was delivered, and to whom Jesus said, 'Now go, and tell people what I have done for you.' "

It's true. Regina is not a trained speaker. Her speech would betray her even if she tried to impress her audience. She talks slowly, carefully weighing her words; her grammatical usage reveals no affected polish. Some of her expressions are a carryover from her days as a skid row derelict. But her words are well chosen and clearly convey what she wants to tell her audiences.

Memories flicker in her eyes, and the pain of remembered deeds sometimes causes her to pause. But her past experiences give her rapport with those who listen to her. They sense that

23

she knows and understands their problems, their situations, and that she can truly identify with them. And God uses this identity to touch hearts and soften spirits. Regina Ramsay is his vessel—filled to overflowing with God's love.

Regina's father was a six-foot-five Irishman from West Virginia, the third of her mother's five husbands. The six children were raised on corn liquor, smoking, cussing and fighting. Because of alcohol and misery, the children did not receive proper care. When she was seven, Regina's father died. Regina's mother did not stay a widow for long—within the year she had remarried. The children had never heard the name "God" or "Jesus Christ" except as a swear word. But their new grandmother, a devout Roman Catholic, succeeded in getting these children eight months of religious training. Regina learned that Jesus Christ had hung on a cross, she memorized prayers, knew she had sinned, and knew that she could confess her sin, but she never experienced peace. She did not know that she could take her sins to Christ, that she needed to be born again, or that she should read the Bible. Life, even as an eight-year-old, was a terrible turmoil.

When Regina was ten, her mother divorced this fourth husband and left Regina with another family. "There were so many kids, dogs and cats around I don't think they really knew I was there until they asked me to leave when I was almost thirteen," she says.

What do you do when you are barely thirteen, and all alone in the world? You go looking for your mother, even if your memories of that mother are anything but good. Regina found her in Sacramento, California—married to another alcoholic. In a very short time her mother again abandoned her. This time she, along with her husband, went to Portland, Oregon. Regina stayed in Sacramento, which, at that time, had one of the toughest skid rows in the state.

Hungry, deserted, alone—the pretty, dark-haired girl, tall for her age, went where food was cheap. She found other young people her age who, likewise, had been pushed out onto the streets. Skid row became their habitat. Under such circumstances she learned early to hate. For the most part, the people with whom she found herself were Mexicans, Chinese, Filipinos,

Negroes, Puerto Ricans and gypsies. They decided to form a family. Now, as she looks back, she realizes they were a gang. Tough? To all appearances they were, but underneath they were a bunch of little kids scared to death. They hung to each other—hoping that by acting tough they wouldn't get hurt.

She started drinking at thirteen because the only answer to problems that she had ever been given or shown was—drinking. Drinking was the way to celebrate. It felt good to drink. If you were sad, drink. Problems? Drink. Drink, and cry in your beer. By the time she was seventeen she was what Alcoholics Anonymous call a potential total alcoholic and narcotics user.

While roaming the Sacramento streets, she met and married a boy of eighteen because he had five hundred dollars. She thought they were rich! The marriage didn't last, but by the time he left her she was pregnant. Fifteen and pregnant! She had been told never to trust anyone, especially men. Now she felt she knew firsthand.

Homeless and hungry Regina put in a call to her mother. "She sent me $20 for the fare to Portland. A baby boy was born. When my little boy was fifteen months old, my mother demanded custody of him, told me I was no good, and kicked me out. If it had been up to the courts to decide, both of us would have lost him. I was angry, and decided I'd show her. I'd make a lot of money and then she'd accept me. So would everyone else. Money would make the difference. Money meant happiness didn't it?"

Thoroughly convinced that she was no good, Regina returned to Sacramento, and skid row—and the only way of life that she knew. There she made money by getting into the rackets. She started out at $20 a day. Sometimes she made $200 to $300 in a single day! But she didn't save a dime because she wanted everyone to know she had money. In her desire to be recognized and flashy, she would throw hundred dollar bills over the bar counter. At seventeen, she had a new car, diamonds, clothes and plenty of spending money. She literally went from rags to riches.

"Conning" the suckers, "scoring for a meal or man," "hustling," living on beer and whiskey, and getting her thrills from marijuana: these activities made up Regina's life. Dealing in the rackets on skid rows in many big cities took her as far east as Chicago. Out of this life a daughter was born when Regina was eighteen.

"I know now it was only by God's grace that the child survived. No one had ever taught me how to take care of a child. I dragged her around the country like a rag doll. She became everything to me. I loved her; she was mine. But she was always sickly. I fed her only when I felt like eating. I knew nothing about formulas and baby care. She didn't have her first baby shot until she was five."

A turning point in Regina's life came when she met a man twenty years her senior. He was an intellectual, an atheist who had been dabbling in psychology for fifteen years. "When he met me, he figured he'd have a field day," she recalls with a sad half-smile. But the importance of the relationship was that the man convinced her she wasn't stupid or necessarily worthless. He enrolled her in night school where, motivated by his confidence in her, she worked hard and learned quickly—and her self-confidence grew.

"In my heart I wanted to be decent," she says. Now, with this newly gained self-confidence, she felt she could make a stab at living a normal life. Getting her son back was the beginning. When she regained custody of him, four-years-old by this time, she realized the child had an emotional problem. Marriage would give stability and security. Her children needed a father.

"I went looking for a tall man, one I could manipulate to my own liking, one who loved to dance because I liked jazz, one who would stay home and babysit nights if I wanted to go out drinking, and one who had a steady job," is her confession.

"I didn't know God had anything to do with a marriage, and the word *love* meant merely *to use somebody*. I looked around, sorted out a few possibilities, and came up with one I knew was a prize. Dave Ramsay fell head over heels in love with me. He had a decent family background, a year of college, and seniority of three years with a firm where he worked. We met in December 1959 and were married in March 1960."

Gradually, Dave learned of her lurid past. Loving her, he tried to make up for her past by buying her things. "He bought me a house, car, clothes, furniture and worked twelve, fourteen, sometimes sixteen hours a day to pay for it. I didn't know how to handle money. Then I realized he wanted something besides the physical from me—and something besides a cook and housewife. He wanted a 'feeling.' I didn't have it.

"The children, too, wanted something from me that I didn't have. I felt obligated. Trapped. I drank heavier. We talked of divorce. Then Dave suggested we move to Portland, where I could talk my problems over with my mother and analyze the difficulties—and maybe we could make the marriage work. We salvaged what we could and moved a block from my mother. For two years we drank and cried together about our problems.

"One night my mother phoned and asked me to go out for a drink with her. She was already drunk. I refused to go. She took a bottle of sleeping pills, killing herself. This frightened me. I didn't want to think about it. I wanted to escape."

Regina sought her escape in becoming a career woman. She found a company that would train her. In a year and a half she had worked so hard and done so well that she became department head. But she was still miserable. During the week she would work until she was exhausted, and then spend her weekends drinking. Her children and husband were neglected. Her eleven-year-old son—who stole, lied, and bullied others— was considered a delinquent. The two little girls (a girl was born to the Ramsays during their first year of marriage) were emotionally upset. Terribly discouraged, but still wanting to find the answers to their problems, Regina and Dave decided to try guidance counseling. They sent their son to a Child Guidance Clinic; Dave attended a therapy group; and Regina went to a counselor. She felt things would improve—after all, wasn't psychology supposed to be the answer to everything?

But improvement did not seem very rapid. On the day before Christmas, Regina got up, sluggishly walked to the window and looked out at Mt. Hood. Her mother's body had been cremated and the ashes scattered over the mountain. Her mother had said she wanted to be free—to float in the breeze. Regina wondered if her mother was free. She, too, wanted to be free. She was tired of people and circumstances.

Thoughts of suicide had been in Regina's mind for a long

time, but she was afraid to die. That morning she picked up a bottle of sleeping pills, and as she stood there looking at them, a wave of despair came over her. In desperation she cried out, "O God, give me the courage to take these pills."

When she called out the name, "God," something seemed to go out of her. She couldn't see it, but she sensed it. She knew it was rotten and in its place something else came in. Words, in the form of a song, came from her lips: "I want to walk in the arms of the Lord."

From that moment her life began to change. Immediately she was overcome with the desire to confess her sins. At work she sought out a fellow employee who talked often of his church. "Don, I'm going to give myself a Christmas present, I'm going to go to church." He encouraged her by saying he'd done the same thing some time before and his life had been changed. "Regina," he urged, "let my pastor come talk to you."

When the pastor called Regina blurted out her experience. He encouraged her to attend their church and extended an invitation for that Sunday night.

Regina told her husband and they decided to take the children. Her son, openly incredulous, said, "Are we going to church? Man, I'm not going to church!"

Regina answered, "Shut up." She stuck a belt in her purse—and they all went!

The church was full. When the congregation started to sing, Regina thought the roof would come off. But as she joined in the singing, Regina says she had her first inkling of joy in twenty-eight years. Afterwards everyone shook their hands and made them feel welcome.

When they were invited to the church for an old time revival Regina thought, "Oh boy, this is where everybody will act crazy, it ought to be interesting." So, out of curiosity they went.

The speaker began by saying, "I came here tonight to tell you all about sin. . . ." Regina thought, "Man, I know all about sin."

The speaker continued, "I know more about sin than anything else. This is something I can really talk about. I used narcotics, booze, women and anybody who got in my way. But one day I found out that Jesus Christ could give me a different feeling and take away my sin. When I found out about that I decided to let God use me. . . ."

Regina's mind was spinning! "This is where you go to confess—to Jesus Christ. But, where is he? I know he was born in a manger, and that you sing Christmas carols about him. I know he hung on a cross." And then she really began to listen.

On the third night of the revival meetings when the invitation was given, one of Regina's daughters was the first person to go forward. Immediately her son followed. Regina watched them, particularly her son, and thought, "This is good, whatever it is. I'll follow him so he won't turn around and sit down." Her husband immediately followed her.

The counselors took them in separate rooms and asked them to pray. "I had never prayed out loud before, and I was scared. I said the first thing that came to my mind: 'God, I give my son to you.' That night my son did give his life to Jesus Christ—and he never went back to the Child Guidance Clinic. Up to this time his report cards had been so bad they couldn't even grade him. The first report card he got after accepting Christ was remarkable. I knew something had happened to my boy that night—even though I hadn't accepted Christ myself."

Regina and her husband started attending a Bible class. Of the leader she says, "He was eighty-one years old, and eighty-one years wise in the Lord. We had 5,000 questions, and he had 5,000 answers."

One day this venerable old saint said to Regina, "You can ask questions from now until doomsday, and you'll never understand this Bible and Jesus Christ until you ask him into your life."

Regina's answer was prompt, and typical of her: "How can I ask someone into my life who lived and died 2,000 years ago?"

With loving kindness and an infinite patience the old gentleman explained, "The Father, the Son and the Holy Ghost are all one. They form the Godhead. The Father allowed a man to be born, and he breathed his spirit into this man. This man, Jesus, lived a perfect life; he did not commit any sin for which he had to die. But he willingly died and shed his blood for you and me. His blood redeems you and everybody else in this world from sin when you (and they) confess their sin and accept his gift of salvation. For a short time, Jesus came back to life to defeat death and to show people he was God. Then he went to the Father and sat at the right hand of the Father in Heaven. When you ask Christ to forgive you and help you live as he lived, and as the Bible teaches, he sends the Holy Spirit to live in you. . . ."

Regina went home. She thought about these things for four months. During this time she did not take even one drink. Then one night, in a bleak, angry mood, she got into her car intending to go for a drink at some bar. Instead, she drove to the deserted graveyard not far from their home. Feeling miserable, worthless, without hope, she looked down at the lights of the city, her mind in a discouraged muddle.

"Jesus," she prayed, "if you are real, if you can really forgive me for my sins—and you know I've done everything short of killing someone, I've even used a knife on people—come into my heart, send your Holy Spirit. I don't have anything to lose. If you can't do it, I'm going to kill myself."

Immediately, she experienced peace. She became very calm. She felt no excitement, only peace and the longing to go home. When she got home, she didn't say anything, but the peace of mind and heart continued. That night she slept soundly. When she awoke, she knew her experience of the previous evening was real—she knew she'd been born again.

Then she shared her experience with her family. She was thrilled that God could touch her even though she couldn't see him.

She worked with three girls who complained constantly so she said to them: "Don't you know, Jesus Christ can help you?"

Their answer was a horrified, "Now Regina, don't get fanatical, you'll lose all your friends!"

Regina thought about that. To herself she said, "Now look, those friends didn't give you peace or eternal life. What do you care what they think?"

From that time on she was concerned only about Jesus Christ. Years before she had stolen a Bible, now she started reading it. And her prayer became, "O God, I want to see everyone saved!"

In her fervor she spoke to everyone she knew and met. But, disappointed with their responses, she sought out the counsel of the wise leader of the Bible class. "Everytime I mention the name Jesus Christ I lose a friend!"

Joyfully he replied, "Praise the Lord!"

Surprised, Regina exclaimed, "You mean to tell me I'm supposed to praise the Lord everytime I lose a friend?"

The man of God rejoined, "Yes! Everytime you lose a friend, or are persecuted for Jesus' sake, you will be blessed."

Today, Dave and Regina Ramsay, having experienced Christ's indwelling presence, knowing the miracle of being born into God's family, and living in the joy, peace and love which God gives through Christ, are walking hand in hand for him—and their children walk with them in Christ.

They have dedicated themselves to helping derelicts. Mrs. Ramsay has received commendation from former Governor Mark Hatfield of Oregon, and others in the courts, prisons and places where she is asked to tell her story.

There are those who openly jeer, who assail with bitter words and rise up with open rebellion, when Regina speaks. But God is her shield, and he has not given her "a spirit of fear, but of power, and of love, and of a sound mind" (II Timothy 1:7).

Cameo three

Congo Calling Dr. Dix

Ruth Dix

Dr. Herb Atkinson lifted the tiny infant by his heels, slapped its bottom and smiled at his first cry. "You have a boy, Ruth," he said, "and by the sound of things he's going to be all right."

Yvonne Dind, obstetrical nurse, looked over at the waiting father and offered: "And he looks just like you, Rich."

Richard Dix had spent most of these anxious, pre-birth moments with his head in his hands. It had been nearly too much for the new father, but at the mention of his name he snapped back to life. Sitting beside him was his mother-in-law, Dr. Grace King, who had flown from her California home to this missionary hospital in the Congo for the birth of this grandchild.

The thirty-one-year-old woman who had just given birth to her first child had delivered hundreds of babies for others. Now she could only do what other new mothers do, sigh happily and relax, knowing it was over! "It's different all right," she admitted groggily, "being *on* the table."

Outside the mission hospital, Congolese men and women heard the news and spread the word: "Dr. Ruth has just had her baby, a boy ... Dr. Ruth is doing fine, and so is the baby."

In the delivery room, nurse Vera Thiessen cleaned the newborn babe, wrapped him in a blanket and handed him to the nervous father, "Here, Rich, take him out and show him to the Africans."

Richard Dix gently, though rather clumsily, took his little son into his arms and walked outside. When the crowd saw him they let out a loud cheer! At the cry of welcome, Dr. Ruth and her African midwife, Debby, smiled at each other.

When the father and son returned, Dr. Herb said, "OK, Rich, you can take her home now!" And Richard Dix picked up his wife in his arms and carried her to their mission compound home. Grandmother King followed, cradling the baby in her arms. It had been a very wonderful, unforgettable experience.

Later that afternoon fifteen Africans crowded in to see Dr. Ruth and the baby, much to the surprise of some who felt Ruth should stay secluded. "Let them in . . . I want to see them," Dr. Ruth insisted. And in they came, bringing gifts for the baby . . . everything from a flower to a live goat! This was their way of showing the young doctor how much they loved her and wanted to share in her happiness.

She thanked them, happiness welling up to overflow. Yes, it was different in many respects from what it might have been—care in a sterile delivery room with the latest equipment—but she wouldn't have wanted it that way! She knew she was in the right place, though it had taken years to get here!

How does a thirty-one-year-old woman doctor, who could have had a flourishing practice in the United States or chosen any of a number of attractive positions, land in the middle of Africa—and find herself supremely happy?

I asked those questions and I wondered. The answers began to come in the lovely living room of Dr. and Mrs. Marchant King that overlooks California's San Fernando Valley. As I talked with the Kings, I sensed that they, too, could be the subjects of an intriguing story, and that their daughter's fulfillment could be traced back to these parents.

Ruth's story begins in Brooklyn, New York, on December 29, 1934, where she, and later her brother Paul, were born. Her father pastored the Westminister Church in Newburgh, New York, on the Hudson River just above West Point.

When Ruth was three, her father became mysteriously ill. They visited doctor after doctor, and specialists finally told Mrs. King her husband had progressive muscular dystrophy.

What a shock! Marchant King had specialized in Semitic studies at Princeton Seminary, and at the same time, earned a master's degree in Arabic at the university. The future had looked so promising—now the future was draped in financial debt and physical liabilities. Together they sought the Lord's guidance.

Mrs. King surveyed the situation. Prior to their marriage she had been graduated from Barnard College and was a teacher. Now she realized she should return to college and prepare herself further for a teaching career. While her husband continued in the pastorate, she attended New York University while "tripling" as a pastor's wife and a mother. In three years she earned a Ph.D. degree.

To avoid the extreme winters of the Northeast, the family moved to California and Dr. Marchant King began teaching at Culter Academy. Dr. Grace King became head of the English department of Westmont College (then located in Los Angeles).

Busy parents though they were, the Kings took time each day to train their children in Bible truths. Memorization of the Scriptures, keeping notebooks on Bible lessons, and regular family devotions were an absolute must. Ruth and her brother absorbed readily, and enjoyed the variety of ways in which their parents taught and applied the truths of the Word. In later years, Ruth was to look back and credit this teaching in the home as the influence that called her back to the Lord when she might easily have gone another way.

When Dr. King was offered a teaching position at Baptist Seminary and a part-time teaching post at Culter, the family moved to Glendale and Mrs. King joined the counseling staff of Glendale College. Later she became chairman of the Division of Language Arts, a position she retains to this day.

Ruth was graduated as valedictorian of the senior class at Culter. She entered UCLA and completed the pre-med requirements by her junior year. Then, only nineteen, she announced to her parents: "I'm going to take the AMA test for medical school."

Ruth's mother looked at her daughter seriously and replied, "If you start medical school, young lady, you're going to finish!" This was obviously a very important decision.

Ruth carefully weighed her wishes and inclinations and approached her parents again. This time she said, "Why should I waste another year at UCLA when I'm through with all my pre-med requirements? I might go to the mission field some day, and if so, a year would mean a lot as I'd have to take time out for language studies."

Who could argue with such logic? Certainly not the Christian parents of a daughter with ability and high ideals. Application was made to the Woman's Medical College of Pennsylvania. Interviews and correspondence followed. One day when Ruth came home the family rushed out to meet her, waving a letter. She'd been accepted! Ruth put her head down and cried softly, happy but knowing four years of demanding work lay ahead.

At summer's end her parents accompanied Ruth east. Coming from California into the factories and atmosphere of Philadelphia's Germantown, where she was to live, presented quite a contrast. The look on Ruth's face revealed inner conflict. Her mother's gentle reminders that this was God's provision, and that after all, the school took only fifty students a year, turning down applicants from all over the country, reassured Ruth, and she recovered her poise.

The Kings left Ruth at the Keswick Bible Conference in New Jersey, praying it might be spiritual preparation for the years ahead. Later Ruth found warm Christian fellowship at the Plymouth Brethren Assembly in Germantown, and the regular days of prayer she attended at the China Inland Mission headquarters fortified her. Many times Ruth thought of the mission field, but notions of romance and of professional success readily pushed thoughts of missionary work into the vague future. Someday, perhaps.

Then too, she remembered Dr. William Chisholm, medical missionary to Korea; and Dr. Walter Lambie, field director of the Sudan Interior Mission, medical missionary and personal physician to Emperor Haile Selassie of Ethiopia. These missionaries and others had visited in the King home. On many occasions she listened in rapt attention as they talked of their mission work.

The months and years of training slipped by. The summer prior to her senior year, she worked with Dr. Ralph Byron, chief surgeon at the famed City of Hope Medical Center. With his encouragement, Ruth discovered she had a natural flair for surgery. Her senior year was spent largely in clinical work. And then it was time for graduation.

The Glendale *News-Press,* Glendale, California, carried a news item dated June 20, 1959, whose headline read: "Many Honors Conferred Upon Local Woman Graduated From College." It told of Ruth receiving her M.D. degree at Woman's Medical College of Pennsylvania, that she was graduated cum laude, ranked at the top of her class and received the American Medical Women's Association award for the highest average in her class for four years.

Ruth also received the Albert Einstein Memorial Award for superior academic performance, the Professor of Surgery prize for excellence in surgery, and the Merck Citation as outstanding senior of the year!

In medical school Ruth had been active in the Christian Medical Society, and was president her junior and senior years. She was selected to represent the college at the American College of Surgeons convention in Chicago, in October, 1958, and was on a panel in June, 1959, for the American Medical Women's Association in Atlantic City.

Ruth's delighted parents went east for her graduation and for her brother Paul's marriage—a joyful time for the family.

That July Ruth started her internship at Los Angeles County General Hospital—at twenty-three years of age. If other interns and orderlies looked at her with apprehension and doubts, it was no wonder. Not only was she young, but she was perhaps the prettiest intern they had ever seen! Their worries were wasted!

When it came time to allot duty hours, Ruth was told, "We'll take the first three nights, you take the fourth." It dawned on her suddenly that this would be the night of July 4—on the jail ward! Before leaving, the head physician asked, "Ruth, do you think you'll be all right tonight?" Ruth replied, "Of course!"

As she began her duty, an ambulance pulled up and a number of deputies followed the attendants in with a badly slashed patient. It appeared this would be an unforgettable

Fourth of July! An assistant looked bleakly at the young doctor and managed a feeble: "What are you going to do?" Ruth took one look at the stretcher case, fixed her gaze on the attendant, and answered matter-of-factly: "I'm going to sew him up!" If there were any more questions or doubts in the minds of those who worked with Ruth, they were soon dispelled.

That year Ruth determined to take her residency in obstetrics at L.A. County General. When she mentioned this to several co-workers they laughed. "You'll never get it! You're a woman and the competition is terrible." That year, out of eighty-five applying for this residency, five were chosen—Ruth was one of the five! She remained in this position for the next four years.

Those were busy, important years. In her last year, Ruth was in charge of all diabetic pregnancies in the clinic. She also had six months of general surgery. Some days she began at 6:30 in the morning and did not finish until two the next morning. The experience she gained was extensive in many related fields, (enabling her to say several years later: "I haven't seen a case in Africa that I hadn't already seen at County Hospital").

During these years Ruth was conscious that her knowledge of God's Word wasn't affecting her contacts with needy people. When movie actress Marilyn Monroe committed suicide, Ruth was working in the Admitting Room, and in a subsequent four-week period she admitted over one hundred people under thirty years of age who had taken an over-dose of barbituates in the manner of the movie idol. Telling of her experiences later to a Christian group at a Lyceum Eteri Conference Ruth said:

"I looked at these people, most of them attractive young Caucasians, and knew I was being shown something. Many of them, even though successful, were desperately unhappy. They were bitter, cursing the fact they hadn't died, and furious with themselves for failing and with the doctor who had stepped in to save them from death.

"When I went off duty that night, I thought, 'The boys on medicine are really going to be busy tonight!' But the crux of the matter wasn't that the doctors were going to be busy; there was a terrible lack of purpose in many lives. I began to think: What am I really doing with *my* life? How much is it counting for God?

"I thought about that for several days, but then the sense of purpose passed into the background as I was extremely busy in obstetrics and I found the abortion patients particularly pathetic."

Ruth's heart went out to the young, bleeding girls. Many of them died of infection in spite of her efforts to pull them through.

"Many times I would talk to them and ask, 'Why?' They would lie to me with straight faces, 'No, I wasn't pregnant. . . .' Others would say, 'I don't want children; I've had it bad enough myself and I don't want to bring children into the world to live like this.'

"God was speaking to my heart again, pointing out the degradation of sin, the desperateness of lives that didn't know the Lord Jesus Christ. But, once again, it got to the point where it bothered me only temporarily.

"And then, in the fall of 1963, I was brought up short by the realization that in July of 1964 I would be finishing my residency at L.A. County. I knew I faced a major decision, and whatever I decided had to be right because it involved the rest of my life. I knew God's Word well enough to realize if I missed his will I'd be miserable. I had to admit I was frightened over making that decision.

"When it came time to make that decision, three avenues were open to me: First was the academic field. My own medical school had offered me a faculty position and also a part-time practice with the Head of Obstetrics and Gynecology at Woman's. It was a very attractive offer and I went back and looked it over. Or I could be on the staff at the University of Southern California.

"Possibility number two was private practice, settling down in Southern California in partnership or alone. There were lots of opportunities.

"Possibility number three was the mission field. Had God put me through all this medical training so that he could use me full-time on the mission field?

"In the midst of this dilemma one day the phone rang. It was Dr. Byron at City of Hope. We had kept in touch since my work there, and he had taken a real interest in my training. He was very direct: 'Ruth, I want you to come out to the City of Hope. I think you need it. This would be good finishing up for your training, and besides that I think you need it spiritually.'

"Frankly, I didn't know what to say. I knew he was right, but I didn't want to admit it. I had been under lots of strain and in charge of two hundred patients and twenty to thirty doctors. I knew Dr. Byron well enough to know he'd spent much time in prayer about it. I also remembered another time in my life when, in talking with him, he'd brought up a problem in my life that I'd never mentioned to him. God directed this man in what he said.

"And so I had answered him, 'Another year in training? I've already had five.' He had answered, "You'd better come out here and talk to me.'"

She went to see Dr. Byron, and the essence of their conversation was the same as it had been over the phone. At the end of three weeks she made up her mind and called him to say, "Yes."

In times of temptation and rebellion, Ruth's thoughts always turned to God's Word. She couldn't get away from the early home training and from the verses she had memorized through the Navigator program. And, working side by side with Dr. Byron, she was brought back into daily, deep fellowship with Christ. Her prayer and quiet times were renewed, and she accepted a Bible class leadership with student nurses at L.A. County Hospital.

Ruth also started attending the Church of the Open Door in downtown Los Angeles. There she met Richard Dix, who, she discovered, knew many of the same people she did. Richard's parents were missionaries with the Africa Inland Mission in the Congo. Richard had been offered a job in New York as a construction engineer, but he had come to Los Angeles for a year's experience before going back to Africa under appointment of A.I.M.

The friendship grew between Ruth and Richard, but both realized another Christian young lady was involved; in fact, the second woman was first in Richard's affections. Ruth discussed the situation seriously with her mother, an experienced counselor as well as a godly mother, and Ruth decided she would not see Richard again. "This was not an easy decision because Richard and I had become very attracted to each other," Ruth relates.

More and more the mission field was creeping into Ruth's thinking. She felt definitely that she shouldn't go back to Woman's in Philadelphia. She had visited medical missions in Central America and the Orient. She wondered about the value of seeing medical work in Africa and India.

"I asked Dr. Byron for a month's leave of absence to visit these fields, and he was enthusiastic. He suggested I also visit Ethiopia, Egypt, the Holy Land and Copenhagen, Denmark. I laughed and told him I couldn't possibly do all that in four weeks, and he said, 'Take six.' The Lord opened the way and on October first, while I was somewhat afraid to trust the Lord, I left by Pan American for New Delhi, India."

From New Delhi, Ruth went to Multan in West Pakistan, where she spent five days with Dr. Alice Kitchen, then on to the Congo to fulfill a pledge to help for three weeks. Next she moved to Ethiopia where her late beloved Dr. Lambie had served, and then to Egypt. She crossed to Israel, where she was met by Mr. and Mrs. Henry Medrow with the Plymouth Brethren mission, and stayed briefly at Nazareth. She toured some of the Holy Land, and then hopped to Greece, Rome, and Copenhagen. Wherever she went, she had letters of introduction to medical doctors, and so she saw the vast scope of medical work in these parts of the world. It was a tremendously valuable experience.

But in Africa something happened which was to alter her life. She was met in Nairobe by missionary doctor Bill Barnett who had been told he was to pick up an American medical doctor, a woman. When Ruth stepped off the plane, Dr. Bill thought, "I can't believe it! This young woman is a surgeon?"

The rugged trips into the bush county and limited working facilities were a severe test of Ruth's endurance and adaptability. She passed the test, and while there God unmistakeably spoke to her heart: "This is where I want you."

Once again, memorized Scripture came to Ruth's mind and reassured her: "Casting all your care upon him; for he careth for you" (I Peter 5:7); "be not conformed to this world; but be ye transformed by the renewing of your mind, that ye may prove what is that good, and acceptable, and perfect, will of God" (Romans 12:2).

She knew God was saying to her, "This is my reasonable, intelligent, good will for you." She had looked over varied mission fields, and God did not speak to her in this way until she reached the Congo. Joy and peace flooded her heart.

As Ruth stepped off the plane in Los Angeles, she was met by a crowd of friends and her family. As she looked over the group, she saw a familiar face: Richard Dix was among the greeters! No one could have been more surprised than Ruth when her mother told her that night that Richard had changed his plans. She gasped in disbelief and hope and said, "The Lord couldn't be that good!"

The friendship between Ruth and Richard deepened from that moment. Ruth had no way of knowing that while she was receiving God's call to Africa, Richard's affections had shifted. They were together again to follow God's will in partnership.

In June 1965, Ruth and Richard were married. It was a beautiful wedding, but the newlyweds' hearts shone more than their finery. Ruth says, "What the Lord did for us was extra-special. Only a God of great grace could have drawn us so wonderfully together."

They left for Switzerland at the end of August to begin six months of intensive language training. Word reached them from Dr. Carl Becker* in Nyankunde, Congo, that he was alone at the medical center and needed Ruth desperately. So, leaving earlier than expected, Ruth and Richard flew to Congo.

Arriving at Nyankunde on a Thursday afternoon, Ruth had a sudden initiation into her work as Dr. Becker left on a medical trip Friday morning and gave Ruth full responsibility for the hospital. With no grasp of Swahili and a medical situation very different from that of County Hospital or City of Hope, she began her life as a medical missionary with the calm assurance that she was in God's place—a place for which he had specifically prepared her.

---

*Dr. Becker's life story is told in *Another Hand on Mine,* published by McGraw-Hill, written by William J. Petersen.

Their days became a kaleidoscope of activity. Rich works steadily at rebuilding property damaged and destroyed by the Simbas in the uprisings of 1964. The Becker home, duplexes for missionaries, a new chapel, a dispensary, new water system, their own home and many other projects have taken form under his skillful hands.

Days never seem long enough for Ruth as she works with Dr. Becker, Dr. Helen Roseveare,** Dr. Atkinson, and the nurses and native workers. Infirmiers screen the long lines of patients, treating the less serious ones, and somehow ministering to 1,200 to 1,800 a day! In addition to her duties at the hospital, Dr. Ruth conducts a well-baby clinic once a week, helps the women who have difficulty in childbirth or with sterility, and assists in the training of Congolese obstetrical nurses and medical students. On Sundays the medical staff holds evangelistic services in nearby villages.

It was a happy reunion for the Dixes and Dr. Grace King when the latter arrived to welcome Ruth and Richard's first child, Stephen Paul.

A few days later, as a national was holding the baby, someone said to Ruth, "You're letting them hold your baby? Why, I never let them hold my babies!" Ruth smiled, looked lovingly at her firstborn and the national holding the child, and answered, "Why not? I hold theirs!"

Indeed she does. For this is Dr. Ruth Dix at work in the Evangelical Medical Center of Northeast Congo. Delivering babies, performing surgery, talking to her patients in Swahili, and to her nurses in French, wherever she now goes, whatever she does, it is with the sure knowledge that God, by his grace, is working with her.

The present and the future belong to her heavenly Father. Richard and Ruth confidently accept each new day, asking only that "they might be to the praise of his glory" (Ephesians 1:12).

**Dr. Helen Roseveare's life story has been told in books published by Christian Literature Crusade and Wm. B. Eerdmans Publishing Co.

Cameo four

Double Trouble-- Double Triumph

Joyce Landorf

Razor blade in hand, preferring death to the awful struggle of living a life of pretense, Joyce Landorf paused at the sharp ring of the phone. She trembled, sharp blade on her wrist. "No one has any answers for me," she thought. "Why don't they let me alone?" The caller was persistent, the phone kept ringing. Feeling beyond the place of being hurt or helped, Joyce picked up the phone and said, "Hello."

"Joyce," said the caller urgently, "I don't know what you are doing, but whatever it is stop and listen to me!"

Joyce was furious! She recognized the voice of a minister friend and she resented the intrusion.

Not waiting for an answer the caller continued, "Firmly grasp what you know to be the will of God, Joyce. I know you're in no mood to listen, but the Bible says, 'Having done all, to *stand.*'"

He was talking quietly into the receiver when Joyce slammed it down. Stunned, she walked back to the bathroom and picked up the razor . . . and then the enormity of what was happening reached her. Putting down the blade, she found herself questioning, "God, God, do you care about me?"

The words the caller had spoken were from the Bible, and they meant the difference between life and death for the distraught wife and mother. As she hesitated, questioning God, the words of a Bible verse she had learned as a child came to her: "The Son of man is come to seek and to save that which was lost" (Luke 19:10).

Severed from the despair and anguish of the preceding moments, Joyce walked into her living room and dropped on her knees by a chair to pray. . . .

Across the city at the same time Dick Landorf was nurturing hateful thoughts about his wife Joyce. Bitterly he took a pen and began writing it all out—his last, venomous act before he destroyed his life—and then God stopped him. . . .

When Joyce arose from her knees two hours later, she was sanctified, cleansed, forgiven! Never again would terror, doubts and fears control her life. God had met her, showing her that she had rebelled against him, her parents, husband, home and children. Tenderly she had experienced his love and peace as she confessed her rebellion.

What circumstances drive a person to the brink of such despair that suicide seems to be the only recourse? Joyce recognizes that one does not decide quickly to commit suicide. In her case it was a combination of many things. But first and foremost, she came to realize, it was because she did not know Jesus Christ in the personal way that brings purpose and peace to life.

"Having arrived at the failure of my marriage after five years of trying to wear a happy mask," Joyce recalls, "I concluded that I would never be successful. I felt I had failed as a wife, as a mother and most certainly as a singer. When my marriage failed I blamed my husband. When my singing career failed, I could only blame my children and my home duties. But on the day I arrived at the crisis, God began to show me in a thousand ways the real problem was my rebellious self.

"As I look back, it is a terrible thing to think that I was so desperate that I would consider suicide; but if this is where God had to bring me in order to reach me I shall be eternally grateful."

And grateful she is. Bubbling over with gratitude and enthusiasm, the Joyce Landorf of today is a new person in Christ. Have the circumstances changed? Are there no more problems, anxieties, trying moments?

Of course there are cares and pressures. The demands on Joyce's time alone would sink a person of lesser strength. Frail physically, yet a tower of strength spiritually, Joyce meets perplexities, problems, and appointments with the joy and confidence that have characterized her life since that glorious day in 1957.

She says, "Probably the greatest thing Christ did, aside from forgiving me, was to help me forgive myself. Our Lord told us to love our neighbor as our self, and it is most difficult to love one's neighbor if one has no self-love. So, in the early months of my newfound walk with Christ, God helped me to forgive myself and then to claim Paul's words, 'I can do all things through Christ which strengthened me.' You can imagine how much this verse would mean to someone who had failed in everything she had attempted."

When the miracle took place in Joyce's life, transforming her outlook and cleansing her within, a quiet peace and confidence took over. The first question she asked herself was, "But what about Dick? Can love once dead live again?"

The marriage of Dick and Joyce Landorf was on the rocks. She hated her stubborn, good-looking husband. "A handsome husband, two lovely children, and a singing career should be enough to make any woman happy, but I was neurotic and miserable. We had been married only five years; it seemed like fifty.

"Try as I did, I couldn't get it through Dick's head that I was talented, creative, sensitive, and musical, and that I was meant to be vivacious, charming and appreciated. He insisted that I should be satisfied to care for the children, wash dishes and clean the house.

"We had started our home, we thought, on the basis of love for God. We were both active in the church, but before long neither of us was talking with God. In fact, we weren't talking to each other. We had both retreated into our private little world, evading discussion of the real issues that were destroying our marriage and ourselves. I was filled with hate. Dick was consumed, likewise, with hate. We both were so disgusted with living that suicide seemed the only way out."

On the exact day Joyce found Christ as her Savior, Dick came to him also. Joyce was cooking supper when Dick came home that evening. He immediately walked over to her and said, "Joyce, I experienced a miracle in my heart today. I had locked the office door and wrote you a letter filled with hate. I was thoroughly defeated. On the envelope I wrote, 'To Joyce: when you find this I will be dead.' But as I sealed that letter, it was as though God said to me, 'Dick, suicide is not the answer; I am. I am all you need. I will give you abundant life!' "

Life abundant! The words sounded too beautiful to be true. In the shelter of Dick's arms, surrounded by God's love, Joyce knew that life abundant could be a reality. Together they wept. Together they rejoiced as Joyce told Dick what had happened to her that day also. Together they thanked God and pledged their marriage to him.

Joyce had been born in a Christian home. In fact, her father is a minister and her childhood and teen years were spent in the parsonage and church. The legalistic views of the church were responsible for a part of her rebellion; a headstrong fifteen, Joyce told her mother, "Let me love God in my own way; I don't want to be a Christian fanatic."

Patiently and lovingly Joyce's mother pointed Joyce to Christ, and the parents' daily prayers followed her.

Friends called Joyce a multi-talented person ever since she was a little girl. "It has only been since I came to Christ that the talents have been workable or useable," she says.

Career and a man she could love: those were the two things at the top of Joyce's list for a happy future. "I loved music and even before reaching my eighth year I knew I wanted to be a concert pianist. I wasn't going to leave God out—and yet I did. I sang and played in church, but I was trying to get by on my parents' salvation. Christianity, for me, consisted of the common list of do's and don'ts."

When Joyce and Dick married in 1952, Joyce dreamed of a happy future combining a musical career with marriage. The dream was to begin splintering fourteen months later when blue-eyed Ricky put in his appearance. Two years after that, lovely Laurie joined the family. It wasn't that Joyce didn't love her children, but diapers, dishes and drudgery quickly sapped her high-strung strength.

Following Dick and Joyce's reconciliation in May 1957, many things began to change. "To my utter amazement," she said, "I began to enjoy cooking, cleaning and the routine tasks that I had so resented. All of this and mothering my children became a challenge.

"Before Christ, I had all of the reasons for divorcing Dick; after Christ, I was amazed to see God take each objection and turn it into an asset. Together we began studying God's Word, regularly attending church and just growing together in Christ.

"This reflected on our attitudes toward the children. Our children are very precious to us and a continual joy to our hearts. As parents, we have only one goal for them, that they grow up to be the man and woman God wants them to be. Whatever other achievements they attain are relatively unimportant in comparison with the goals God has for them."

In Southern California, where Joyce is weil known and sought after as a speaker, pianist and vocalist, her dedicated talents have obviously been brought under the control of a Master Hand. Using her formal dramatic training and her ability to compose music and sing has brought Joyce into contact with thousands of individuals with whom she shares her life-changing experience. There is no reticence or shame in speaking of the miracle that occurred in her life. She recognizes that in every audience there may be some who have reached the low ebb that she did.

The most serious problem Joyce now faces is the most profitable use of her time. In addition to being a wife and mother, she has a daily radio program, is women's editor of *The King's Business* magazine, sings for recordings, is a soloist on the TV program *World of Youth,* co-teaches an eleventh grade Sunday school class with her husband and had her first book published in 1968.*

Frayed nerves and nagging family problems might easily arise from such a schedule, but this is not the case in the Landorf household. In fact, so devoted to her home and family is Joyce that she sews all of her daughter's clothes and most of her own. In addition to this, she makes many lovely and practical

Let's Have a Banquet published by Zondervan.

objects for her home and as gifts to friends.

Her explanation of the new smoothness is simple. "I am first a wife and mother. Several years ago I prayed and then talked many hours with my husband about concert schedules, radio broadcasts, personal appearances and time spent in writing. It was then that *my* ministry ceased to exist and *our* ministry began. As I prayed about this, God definitely showed me that I must be a wife first, a mother second, and a singer (or writer, etc.) last. The very moment I began being what God wanted me to be—a wife and mother—the other things fell into place. If I reverse the order or change it, no time is left for even living, much less for a ministry."

So faithful has God been to Joyce that her close friends will tell you that even though she is undoubtedly the busiest mother on the block she knows her children better, plays more games with them and knows more about their lives than any mother with a far less demanding schedule. Laughter and fun, family devotions and reading the Bible together are all a part of the Landorf family life.

On several occasions I have been in an audience where Joyce, with her lovely voice, fingers flying over the keyboard, and beautiful Christ-controlled personality held us spellbound. God has taken her through deepest sorrow, traumatic emotional conflict, and she has emerged a choice "cameo" of his designing.

As she reaches out to share her new life in Christ, some people say, "I feel as though you had been peeking in my house and had described my life and marriage."

Joyce answers: "How grateful I am to God for letting me relate the Gospel in a practical way. It seems incredible that anyone could grow up in a minister's home and not know Christ, but that is exactly what happened to me and is happening to thousands of third- and fourth-generation Christians. I knew all "about" Christ, but I was not his child until John 1:12 took place in my own experience—'But as many as received him, to them gave he power (the right) to become the son (or daughter) of God, even to them that believe on his name.' "

Cameo five

Queen of The West

Dale Evans Rogers

Much has been said and written about Dale Evans Rogers and her husband Roy, but the whole story has not been told. Two million people have bought the eight books Dale has written, and countless millions have watched television and film performances by the "Queen of the West" and "King of the Cowboys," but these multitudes have only begun to get acquainted with Dale and Roy. The truth is that this unique couple's story cannot be captured on paper or film—it is a moment-by-moment, everyday adventure of following God and seeing what wondrous new thing he is going to do.

Dale Evans, cowgirl heroine of thirty-five films with the singing, hard-riding, straight-shooting Roy Rogers, married her co-star on New Year's Eve in 1947. They had worked with each other in the most trying circumstances of "picture-making," and Dale confides: "I saw in Roy a down-to-earth, humble quality that endeared him to people of all ages and circumstances. He was definitely a real person, not a phony. He said what he thought, and could be depended on for an honest answer. I respected this in him."

When Dale married Roy it was to become not only his wife but the mother of his three children. To Roy's home, Sky Haven, Dale brought her twenty-year-old son, Tom Fredericks Fox. When Roy and Dale returned from their honeymoon, she encountered a hostile seven-year-old Cheryl, a brooding four-year-old Linda, and a fifteen-month-old baby, Roy, Jr., called Dusty.

The emotional upsets of those first weeks required every bit of patience, imagination and love Dale could muster. She did everything she could to please the children—playing games, sitting in on music lessons, taking them to their mother's grave, conferring with teachers. All that a mother can do, Dale did, but she sensed the children had not accepted her though they were less troublesome. She longed for their love in return for the love she gave to them.

The love between Roy and Dale deepened with each passing day. To Tom Fox, Dale's son, this was an answer to prayer. Tom, at the time of the marriage, was studying music at USC in Los Angeles. Tom was a devout Christian and had been since he was ten years old. But Tom worried about the Rogerses' children and prayed that the situation would improve.

One afternoon Tom found his mother staring into space in her room and he asked her solemnly: "Don't you want to talk about it?"

"I'm so confused," she said, "that I don't know if I'm afoot or horseback ..." and she poured out her feelings about the new family to her son. She ended by saying in perplexity: "There's everything in this house to make people happy."

"No, Mother, you're wrong," Tom answered. "The loving Spirit of the risen Christ and the wisdom of Almighty God are not in this house. Why don't you start the children in Sunday school? All kids need the kind of security that only real faith can bring." Dale stared at her son in amazement.

"Think back over the years, Mother. Things might have been a lot different for me if I hadn't given my life over to Christ and started asking for his will to be done."

In the hours that followed Dale did lots of thinking. She recalled when she, at the age of ten, had trusted Christ as her Savior. But she knew that, unlike young Tom, she had not put Christ first in her life nor had she followed him in daily living. With regret she recalled the sad consequences—the elopement in her teens that produced an unhappy marriage, desertion, divorce and a deep bitterness. She wished with all her heart she could erase the memories of the following years, but the thoughts continued to come.

She had determined to make good as a professional singer, but the road was rocky. Support of Tom was a major concern, she had to make detours in her career—a business course, a secretarial job—as survival became a driving motivation.

Still she wrestled with her desire to crash big-time radio. She moved from Texas to Chicago, and then, depressed by loneliness and dreadfully ill, she returned to her parents' farm near Dallas. A second marriage followed—and a second failure.

The nagging ambition to be a successful singer hounded her, taking her to a radio job in Louisville, Kentucky. Then a popular program in Dallas auditioned Dale and she clicked. She sang with the orchestras of Ligon Smith and Herman Waldman in the Texas area, along with her radio job. Then she got a chance to sing with Jay Mill's orchestra at the Edgewater Beach Hotel in Chicago. In subsequent years she sang with Anson Week's orchestra and with Caesar Petrillo and his orchestra on the CBS network in Chicago.

In 1940, Dale was asked to make a recording with a Western musical group, The Sons of the Pioneers. That was the day she first heard of Roy Rogers, the singing cowboy of Hollywood.

Dale's talents included the writing of song lyrics. It impressed The Pioneers, but at a night club in Chicago where Ethel Shutta and Ray Bolger were headliners Dale's appearance went over with a thud. The two stars came to Dale's rescue and helped her revise her song, "Will You Marry Me, Mr. Laramie?" and the song went over with a bang.

Hollywood was waiting in the wings, and she went west in the fall of 1941, for screen tests. Twentieth Century Fox signed her, but it wasn't to last long. She met Art Rush who became her agent, and a deep and lasting friendship developed with Art and his wife, Mary Jo. Art introduced Dale to Edgar Bergen, Tony Stanford and Ray Noble whose program was sponsored by Chase and Sanborn. Dale's singing won a long, low whistle from Charlie McCarthy and smiles from the sponsors, and Dale was signed to her first big radio show. She also sang on the Jimmy Durante and Jack Carson shows.

It was the break every career hopeful looks for, but Dale's

happiness was clouded. To promote her chances for stardom Dale had agreed to have her son Tommy pose as her brother. She was living a lie, and hating every minute of it. Her movie debut came in 1943, in *Swing Your Partner* which Dale regarded as a "hayseed musical."

The next assignment caught Dale by surprise—a Roy Rogers western. Republic Studios thought any girl from Texas would know all about horses. Roy regarded Dale with doubt and admiration: he thought she was pretty, but as he said later, "She sure didn't look like a filly who could ride a horse."

Dale hadn't been on a horse since she was seven-years-old, and during the filming Roy teasingly remarked: "I think you're breaking some kind of record, Miss Evans; I've never seen so much sky between a horse and a rider in my life!"

What Dale lacked in horsemanship she made up in determination. When their first picture was released, there was no doubt that a new team had been born. Dale brought real talent as well as beauty to the westerns. Even Roy had to admit this, and her equestrienneship improved steadily.

Dale and Roy's wife Arlene became good friends. Dale respected and admired Roy because of his obvious devotion to his family. Later, when Roy tragically lost his wife, Dale listened sympathetically and offered what help she could.

In her career-climbing days, Dale would never have imagined that stardom could become tiresome. But it did. She became restless and decided to leave westerns—but a man changed her mind! On a rodeo tour in Chicago with Roy's troupe, the star of the show pulled his horse Trigger to a stop beside Dale's Buttermilk and said, "Every king needs a queen." With that he took a tiny jeweler's box from his shirt pocket, removed a small star ruby in a plain gold Tiffany setting and slipped it on Dale's finger.

Columnist Louella Parsons broke the news to movie fans that the future Dale Evans Rogers had a twenty-year-old son. It really didn't matter. Tommy wrote a long letter to his grandparents that expressed his love for the man who was to become his stepfather. But parental and marital love were still not enough to secure happiness in the new family. Dale's thinking, about the past happenings in her life, caused her to make an important decision. She explains it like this.

"I began to realize that this marriage was doomed to failure also as I was no match, alone, for the perils of a Hollywood marriage. So when Tom invited me to attend church at the Fountain Avenue Baptist Church in Hollywood, I went and I heard a searching sermon by Dr. Jack MacArthur on the topic, 'The Home That Is Built On The Rock.' He pointed out that the marriage based on a strong belief in, and commitment to, Jesus Christ would withstand any kind of assault the world had to offer.

"Following the sermon, the minister gave an invitation for people to accept Christ or commit their lives to him. My son spoke to me of my spiritual condition and asked me to commit my life to Jesus Christ in a vital, personal relationship.

"I didn't take the step that day, but the following Sunday I returned to that church and made peace with God through a public stand of confession of faith and a real prayer session with a member of the church. Instantly my life changed. I walked out of that church with my life revolving on a new hub—Christ."

Roy's children accompanied Dale to Sunday school and church and they loved it. Bible reading, memorizing of the Lord's Prayer and the Twenty-third Psalm and other Scriptures, round-the-table grace and singing of hymns around the piano became a part of family devotions in the Rogers household. Dale urged Roy to join them in going to church and in their family devotions.

If the road to stardom was rocky, the walk of faith was strewn with boulders. Dale says, "There were many obstacles to overcome in seeking Christ in a vital way, and endeavoring, by his grace, to follow him. Many critical and disbelieving folks who had known me for years apparently thought I was on some kind of 'religious kick.' They were constantly trying to talk me out of it. Certain practices that had become part of me over the years were almost immediately eliminated through the grace of Christ. I lost the desire for many material things that had meant very much to me before. Some people whom I had counted as friends dropped away. There were many times when I felt quite alone, except for the strong presence of the Lord.

"Roy was not yet a Christian. He was watching me intently. He was not quite sure he liked the abrupt change in me."

Nevertheless, Roy couldn't help but notice the changed atmosphere in his home. The children called Dale "Mom" and there was a beautiful exchange of love. Roy thanked Tom one day for his contribution, and Tom quickly answered, "It wasn't really my idea, Dad. I prayed for guidance and got it." Not long after that the King of the Cowboys started attending church with his family and made his own decision for the Lord.

When Grauman's Chinese Theater in Hollywood asked that Roy's handprint and Trigger's hoofprint be preserved in cement, Pat Brady, Roy's long-time friend, said, "Well, Buck, congratulations! You've just reached the Hollywood pinnacle."

Yes, they had arrived at the top. Fan clubs enrolled some fifteen million members around the world. Products carrying their endorsement were emerging everywhere. And recordings for RCA Victor began skyrocketing, with the songs for children and the hymns and religious numbers especially popular.

Roy and Dale began attending meetings of the Hollywood Christian group. Their old friend Tim Spencer and others helped them immensely in their new walk with God.

When news first spread that the Rogers were expecting a baby, mail from fans flooded in. Not only had their King married their Queen, but now there was to be a Royal Buckaroo!

When the little Buckaroo turned out to be a little Princess, no one could have been happier than Dale and Roy. But their happiness was shortlived with the news that little Robin, as they named their daughter, had characteristics of Mongolism. First to receive the news was Art Rush who, stunned into disbelief, rushed home to tell Mary Jo. Mary Jo sighed deeply and said, "To have Roy and Dale go through so much, God must have in mind for them a great destiny." Those words were to be recalled years later as the impact of Robin's coming, her short life and her inspiring memory accomplished so much for handicapped children around the world.

In the showmanship tradition, the show had to go on, and it did. Roy's and Dale's schedules took them from one end of the country to the other. Wherever they went, they squeezed in visits to hospitals, orphanages and homes for handicapped children. And they were never so busy they couldn't take time to sign their names, pose for photographs, and shake hands.

In Houston, Texas, in 1951 Roy rode out before a stadium audience and network television cameras to sing a new opening number, "Peace In the Valley," a hymn-ballad. A hush fell over the Coliseum arena, and after the song Roy talked to children about the importance of going to Sunday school. It was the first time Roy brought his faith into the public arena, but not the last.

At an adoption home in Dallas, Dale saw a black-eyed, olive-skinned baby girl with coal-black hair. The child was of Choctaw Indian background—the same as Roy's family line. After Dale left the home, the memory of the little "papoose" remained with her.

Little Robin Elizabeth Rogers was laid to rest on the afternoon of her second birthday, August 26, 1952. Their little "angel" was in heaven, and a beautiful peace settled on everyone in the Rogers household.

Dale told the story of little Robin in the book *Angel Unaware,* a little volume which has brought hope and inspiration to millions. In the long days preceding Robin's homegoing, and following her death, Roy and Dale, in her words, were to learn: "The Lord fits the back to the burden. I believe with all my heart that God sent Robin on a two-year mission to our household, to strengthen us spiritually, and to draw us closer together in the knowledge and love and fellowship of God. It has been said that tragedy and sorrow never leave us where they find us ... both Roy and I are grateful to God for the privilege of learning some great lessons of truth through his tiny messenger, Robin Elizabeth Rogers."

Madison Square Garden in New York City was readying for the Rogerses' appearance. Enroute Roy and Dale stopped off at the Dallas adoption home. Spotting the little Choctaw Indian girl, Dale picked her up, hugging her close. "I want this baby, Roy." Before leaving, Roy spoke with officials who promised to consider their request to adopt the child.

The 1952 World Championship Rodeo in New York City gave the Rogerses' troupe an ovation that nearly rocked the building. Roy rode Trigger at breakneck speed into the arena, pulled to a halt and dismounted. He spoke into the mike: "Howdy, pardners," and kids went wild. Quieting them, he went on, "Now, if you please, I'd like to introduce to you a wonderful little gal from Texas who means a lot to me and our kids and does a fine job of keeping a Christian home for us. My wife, the Queen of the West, Miss Dale Evans."

Mary Jo Rush, standing in the wings, was thinking: "There are probably very few people here who remember that Roy and Dale buried the only child of their union exactly a month ago."

Roy then counseled his young admirers: "You go to school five days a week to improve your mind and learn how to be a success in the business world. I want you to go to church one day a week to improve your soul and learn how to appreciate it. The most important thing that ever happened to our family was when we started going to church and began practicing what we learned there. . . . Believe me, pardners, it isn't sissy to go to Sunday school. For, don't ever forget, a real cowboy needs real faith."

The Garden was darkened and spotlights formed a large cross in the center of the arena. A hush fell over the crowd and Roy sang again, "Peace In the Valley" while Trigger knelt nearby as if in prayer. The applause had the roar of thunder.

Back of that witness to their faith lay a weighty decision. Roy and Dale had found peace in God and they were determined to share it. A committee tried to persuade them to drop the religious number, but Dale had said to their manager:

"You know, Art, if you live to get to the top you often forget why you wanted to get there. Roy and I have prayed about this, and we asked God to show us the answer, and he did. If we get booed out of the arena, then that will be that. But .we have decided that the only way to really find ourselves is to lose ourselves in work for others."

They did not get booed out of the arena, and a telegram to their hotel room soon brought the happy news: "The Indian baby is yours." Finishing the New York engagement, Dale and Roy started for home, doing a series of one-night stands on the way.

In Cincinnati, resting before the evening performance, Roy pulled a telegram from a stack of messages and read it silently. That telegram was to lead Roy and Dale to a five-year-old boy, slightly handicapped, who was to walk into their lives on unsteady legs and leave in their arms the next day. Roy had long wanted a boy that age as a companion to Dusty. The child had suffered malnutrition, rickets and curvature of the spine. His nose had been bashed in, evidence of mistreatment. The brave grin on his face went to the hearts of Roy and Dale. He was adoptable. Did they want him?

Together they discussed it. Finally Roy said, "Mama (his favorite endearment for Dale), anybody can adopt a strong, healthy kid who has everything going for him. But what happens to a little guy like this? Let's take him." And take him they did! Thus it was that Sandy joined the Rogers family.

Dale and Roy hit the road for Dallas to pick up the Indian baby. They named her Mary Little Doe, but almost immediately started calling her "Dodie." When Roy and Dale stepped from the plane in Los Angeles with their new children, they were greeted by Dusty, Linda, Cheryl and other relatives, friends, business associates and hordes of photographers, newsmen and fans. There were few dry eyes as Dale came down the steps carrying Dodie and Roy followed with Sandy.

Roy walked over to Dusty, kissed him, and said, "Happy Birthday, son," and introduced Dusty to his new brother Sandy.

Dale went to Cheryl and Linda. "Now we have another baby for our crib, girls."

A newsman said, "Including Tom Fox you now have six children."

"No," answered Dale, "we have seven. Robin is with us now more than she ever was . . . because of her we'll always have more love for all children everywhere."

That love was to stretch out again to an orphanage in Scotland. While in the British Isles, where they had joined Billy Graham on a crusade, they found a thirteen-year-old girl, Marion, a bright, bubbly Scottish-Irish lass who became their foster daughter.

Again, in 1955, Debbie (In Ai Lee), a little Korean-Puerto Rican child from one of the World Vision orphanages in Korea, was placed in the waiting arms of Dale by Dr. Bob Pierce as he stepped from the plane which had carried them so far. The Rogerses had an international family now!

The years moved along—happy, eventful, full-to-the-brim years. Roy and Dale continued numerous appearances with the troupe in many places and countries. Frequently the family accompanied them, joining in singing and performing. Wherever they went, eager arms were outstretched; pitiful little victims of illness and crippling disease looked up at them from hospital beds as they included such visits in their busy itinerary.

They have televised 104 half-hour television films. For four years they did specials for the G M Chevy Show; they have been a part of the Andy Williams show for the past five years; they have been invited to appear on the Hollywood Palace TV show three times; they have done two Telephone Hour performances; appeared with Red Skelton, Kraft Music Hall and other well-known programs.

Honors too numerous to mention have been heaped upon them. In 1967, Dale was named California Mother of the Year; in 1966, Texas Woman of the Year; in 1964, Woman of the Year.

Dale at one time wrote: "I cannot believe that God blunders in sending death. I don't understand all his ways, but I accept them." In 1964, she was to recall those words when Debbie, at age twelve, lost her life in a church bus crash. Dale shared that experience in the book, *Dearest Debbie*. It is a radiant account of the faith that sustained her during the sorrow-filled days after their daughter's tragic death.

When Sandy expressed his desire to enlist in the Army, Roy and Dale gave him their blessing. While serving in Germany in 1965, eighteen-year-old Sandy took a fellow soldier's dare—and lost his life. With the courage that has marked her pilgrimage of faith, Dale told of Sandy, his life, dreams and death in the book *Salute to Sandy*. In memory of their son, and in fulfillment of his dream, Dale and Roy volunteered to perform for the USO. In Viet Nam, they put on shows for military personnel and talked of the peace, power and compassion of God.

Fortune and fame have been matched by pain and sorrow in

the lives of The King and Queen of the West. But all their experiences have tapped a deep reservoir of sustaining faith. Dale sums up their triumphant and tragic experiences by saying:

"Christ has given me a peace that the world does not understand and cannot supply. He has given me a very full cup of life since that wonderful day when I invited him into my heart—a cup of happiness, of sorrow, of purpose, of challenge—and along with these things always his peace that the world cannot take away, regardless of its attacks.

"I feel privileged to have been born into a Christian home and to have had early Christian background and training. With the help of Christ, we have tried to instill in each of our children the truth that Jesus is the Way, the Truth and the Life, and the most important thing in life is to acknowledge him as Lord and Savior. They have been taught to pray daily, to read the Bible, to trust God to guide their lives and to keep their conscience keen and alert to wrongdoing and to pray for his strength to withstand the wiles of Satan. Regardless of the circumstances of one's life, I feel that the truth fits any life and can be applied anywhere.

"We have had, in all, nine children. Six are still living. Five of them are married. We have twelve grandchildren at this writing. As far as I am concerned, there isn't anything in life to compare with a Christian experience. It is stimulating, challenging, wonderful—and has brought me the real happiness of my life. In all the sorrow I have experienced in losing three children, the Lord has always, through his Holy Spirit, comforted my heart and strengthened me, giving me new vision for service. He is, indeed, the Light of my life."

*All of Dale Evans Rogers' books are published by the Fleming H. Revell Company, who have graciously granted permission for this writer to quote from them.

Cameo six

"You May Abound"

Wanda Jones

The dark-skinned attractively dressed woman looked out across the sea of black faces in front of her and gasped in surprise. There were 5,000 women facing her, some with babies cradled on their backs and others weighted down with assorted, colorful bundles. Wanda Jones turned to her companion, Jessie Magill, and asked, "Where did they all come from? How did they get here?"

The veteran missionary looked at Wanda with a touch of amusement and replied, "Most of them walked, some more than forty miles."

Wanda turned again to the huge, outdoor audience. They had trudged many miles to attend the annual conference of Zumuntar Mata, the women's organization of the Evangelical Churches of West Africa. Wanda had thought her own trip was arduous to the Northern Nigeria city, but at least she had ridden all the way, and her back was not bowed by heavy burdens. Now, what would she say to these waiting women? What could she say to this throng whose lives were so different from hers, and who had traveled so far with such high expectations?

Then she knew! Years before, as a student at Nyack Missionary College in New York, God had given Wanda a verse which had been a continual source of strength and help to her.

She smiled at the women, conveying to them, as she had to many, the love she felt for them—the love which binds together all who love Jesus Christ. She was one of them, and they would rejoice with her as she testified that "God is able to make all grace abound toward you; that ye, always having all sufficiency in all things, may abound to every good work" (II Corinthians 9:8).

Yes, *God is able!* Able to take the women of Africa on foot across many miles of dusty trails, with burdens on their backs; able to meet the needs of women in America whose backs may not carry a visible burden but whose very lives are burdens. Women carry burdens the world over, and the Burden-bearer is equally strong and near on every continent.

That conference was one of the most challenging and blessed experiences of Wanda Jones' life. But there have been many times since, just as there had been before that meeting, when she could look up into the face of her heavenly Father, and say, "Thank you God, for your all-sufficiency. . . ."

But how different life might have been for Wanda Jones! How thankful she is that God's enabling grace first brought her to him, and that she recognized his claim on her and surrendered her will. She tells it like this.

* * * * *

I was brought up in a Christian home. I still have vivid memories of my mother mentioning each of her nine children to the Lord in prayer. I remember going to Sunday school and church, and listening to missionaries tell of their experiences; but, I didn't make a definite decision to live for Christ until I was seventeen. My mother died when I was twelve. This made me bitter toward God as I blamed him for taking my mother whom I loved so very much. Her homegoing left an emptiness in my life which, as I grew older, I tried to fill with parties and other activities. This, I thought, would erase the heartache that I so often felt.

I attended special youth services at church one week during the summer of 1940. I had been dating a young man who was an outstanding jazz musician in our city. We were very much in love. We had even made plans to marry after we finished school. It was while he was away playing for a dance in another city that I attended the services which were conducted by the Biola Trumpeters—four young men who were traveling across the country, singing, playing and telling the story I knew so well of Jesus and his love. But that night, as I listened to Chet Padgett, the speaker of the group, tell how Christ and Christ alone could meet the need of one's heart and life, I realized that I needed this Savior desperately.

I got up from my seat as an invitation was given and knelt with other young people. I asked Jesus Christ to come into my heart and life that night. He did just that and gave me such peace and joy. He changed my life and redirected my steps. That night I knew for certain the reality of II Corinthians 5:17 which says, "Therefore if any man be in Christ, he is a new creature; old things are passed away; behold, all things are become new."

Christ changed my life so completely that it had an effect upon the life of Howard Jones, the up-and-coming saxophonist! He congratulated me on joining the church, and since he was already a church member he felt that this would in no way interrupt our plans for the future. But Howard discovered he had never been more wrong.

When Howard proposed marriage, offering me fame and fortune along with himself, I was not swept off my feet as he had expected. I heard myself tell him, "Howard, even though I love you, I love Christ more. Therefore, unless you find Christ as your Savior, I must, for the sake of Christ, leave you because we have nothing more in common with each other."

Howard was really shaken. He tried to convince me that he was just as "religious" as me. After all, wasn't he a member of a church, hadn't he been baptized? He pleaded with me, "Wanda, isn't that enough religion for one man?"

I replied, "It is my personal conviction, now that I am saved, that God has something better for you in life than a career in the dance orchestra business. God has shown me that this jazz orchestra and all that goes with it is not of him. I am going to pray for your salvation, and I am going to also pray that God will soon break up the orchestra."

My heart ached as I looked at Howard. I loved him dearly and I knew he felt such prayers would be the end of him. In reality, they proved to be the real beginning of Howard Jones. Even though he tried to lose himself in his music and the social activity of the jazz world, it didn't bring him the satisfaction he craved. Soon his music began to suffer and the men in his band noticed it. My prayers were being answered as Howard began to realize that without peace in his heart, and without me, music was empty.

When Howard confessed his need of Christ and asked him to come into his life, no one could have been happier than I. When he finally left the band and really began to live for Christ, things began to happen. Howard had his share of joys and troubles too, but God unmistakeably called him into the Christian ministry during this time.

The pastor of our church, Miss Elsie Gatherer, encouraged us both after this to go to a Christian college or Bible school. Howard and I graduated from Oberlin High School in June, 1941. Three months later we entered Nyack Missionary College, Nyack, N.Y. I shall never forget the years spent there in the study of God's Word. Even the trials, problems, and difficulties of campus life were used of God to help mold our lives for the greater challenges of the years ahead.

We graduated from Nyack in June, 1944, and were married. We went to live in New York City, where Howard pastored a church for seven years. Here three of our five children were born. Here God helped and guided us through many joys and heartaches that came to us as a young couple starting out in a big and strange city. After seven busy but wonderful years, we moved to Cleveland, Ohio, where Howard pastored for another seven years.

It was in Cleveland that God gave us a radio ministry over radio station ELWA in Monrovia, Liberia. It was our privilege to travel in Africa in evangelistic meetings for approximately four months in 1957. While there, we felt that God would somehow send us back, but we didn't know when.

In October, 1958, Howard accepted an invitation to become the first Negro associate evangelist on the Billy Graham Team. This meant resigning from the Cleveland pastorate. Howard was to set up the work of the Team known as Operation Africa. And so in 1959 the entire Jones family sailed to Africa. How thrilled and thankful we were! We lived on the compound of Radio Station ELWA, and all of us became involved in producing radio programs in English to reach English-speaking Africans all over the continent.

By this time we had five children: four girls and one boy. I had a program called "Women of Faith"; Howard had a Sunday Bible-teaching program called "Hour of Freedom"; and our children had their own program called "Singtime."

When our three oldest girls, Cheryl, Gail and Phyllis, were seven, five and three years old, I taught them to sing as a trio. The Lord has blessed them through the years, and they are now known professionally as "The Jones Sisters Trio" making recordings on the Word record label, and holding sacred concerts as they continue their college work.

Our son David, fifteen now, has told his father he felt the Lord was speaking to him about preaching the Gospel some day. Whatever course in life David takes, we trust Christ will always be at the center.

Little Lisa is a joy to our hearts. She loves to read, and the Bible is her favorite book.

While residing in Africa, I also taught parttime in our nursery school for missionary children. And it was my privilege to speak from time to time to various women's groups, participate in prayer bands, and speak to young people from elementary age to students of the University of Liberia.

In 1963 we came back to the United States and now live in Oberlin, Ohio. Since then Howard has traveled extensively, both in this country and abroad, conducting evangelistic crusades and Bible conferences with members of the Graham Team. Our broadcasts are still heard weekly across the continent of Africa, and by short-wave they can be heard worldwide. For three years now, I have been teaching retarded children in our community.

Many has been the day in this country and overseas, alone or with loved ones, when I have looked to Christ and been lovingly reminded that God is able. I know that God is interested in every detail of our lives.

I thank the Lord daily for all of his abounding grace to me. In the midst of a world of turmoil and distress I can look around and tell everyone, no matter what the problem, the heartache, or perplexity, and no matter what color skin you have: Give your heart to Jesus Christ and commit your way to him, for *he is able.*

Cameo seven

A Woman of His Word

Marianna Slocum

"What is the price of a Tzeltal New Testament, hermana?"

Marianna Slocum looked at the young man carrying a box of newly printed New Testaments along the jungle trail. Carefully balancing the precious cargo on his shoulder, he eagerly awaited her answer.

"The price of God's Book in your language?" She repeated the question, knowing full well the answer in terms of pesos and centavos. But what about the immeasurable costs paid out in toil, loneliness, single-hearted dedication and even death?

The experiences of the past twenty-five years swirled through Marianna's mind. It was a long way from Philadelphia's Broad Street to the slippery trails, jungle stretches, and sunbaked villages of southern Mexico. Here she had labored with missionary nurse Florence Gerdel and others through the years to win the friendship, trust and the souls of the Tzeltal Indians. And now the Tzeltal Christians who spoke the Bachajón dialect could read God's Word in their own language—and Marianna could rejoice in reaching a long-sought goal.

The distant goal might have taken shape unconsciously, in Marianna's heart during her childhood. Her father, Stephen E. Slocum, brought his family up in the fear of the Lord. Though a civil engineer and university professor who wrote eight textbooks, two historical novels and more than a hundred articles for Christian magazines, he led his family in worship and prayer at every meal. His family of four children remained his first concern and greatest joy.

When Marianna attended college a godly Bible teacher guided her into deeper knowledge of what it means to be a Christian, and Marianna, unknowingly, turned her heart toward a remote Mexican trail.

In her junior year at college, Marianna felt God's leading to translate the Scriptures for a tribe without God's Word. At the same time she heard of Camp Wycliffe, sponsored by the Pioneer Mission Agency of Philadelphia. Marianna decided to apply to this translation organization after graduation.

By the time she was twenty-one, Marianna was eager to follow God's leading. But she first needed to convince her solicitous mother. Jeannette Ware Slocum was a civic-minded, church-going citizen of Philadelphia and a nominal Christian as well as a concerned mother. A severe bout with scarlet fever had left Marianna with a heart defect, and her parents questioned the advisability of Marianna going into rugged missionary work. They asked her to wait a year. Marianna used the delay to take special courses at Philadelphia School of the Bible.

Meanwhile she learned much about the work of the group that was later to be known as Wycliffe Bible Translators. She learned that their primary aim was to go into remote areas of the world where tribes had been isolated for centuries—cut off by language barriers from the rest of mankind, and from God by the fears of heathen beliefs. To give these people God's Word in their own languages, lead them to a knowledge of Christ, and to encourage the establishment of indigenous churches were the goals of the fledgling organization headed by Cameron Townsend.

A further aim of Wycliffe also had great appeal to the keen intellect of Marianna Slocum. Townsend had discovered that a spiritually enlightened people developed a hunger for social and material advancement. So Wycliffe set about to help new Christians become progressive citizens who would be a credit to their communities and countries. Recognizing that the task was tremendous, Wycliffe established the policy that there must be no wasted effort and no duplication of resources and personnel.

The translators, therefore, do not become involved in tasks which other missionary or governmental agencies are equipped to do. Marianna was impressed; the year's wait increased her desire to be a part of such an organization.

In the summer of 1940, Marianna became a part of Wycliffe. One of her first letters during training at Wycliffe Camp gave strong indication that she felt the Lord was leading her to a remote Indian tribe in southern Mexico—the Chols—as a pioneer translator. Her family felt her health was not equal to the task, but rather than oppose her going her parents drove to Camp Wycliffe and then took her in their car all the way to Mexico City! Marianna's heart was touched, and her joy overflowed when her older brother Walter provided the first hundred dollars of her support.

At Camp Wycliffe Marianna had met Bill Bentley, a missionary who began working among Mexico's Tzeltal Indians in 1938. Bill was from Topeka, Kansas, and a graduate of Phillips University. He was preparing to study medicine at the University of Kansas when he came to know Christ in a real way through Bible classes in his home church. Instead of entering medical training he went to Moody Bible Institute. There he heard L. L. Legters describe the need of unreached tribes for the Word of God. Bill attended Camp Wycliffe and then began work among the Tzeltals, descendants of the once-proud Mayans, in Chiapas State.

Bill was a gifted pianist and had a fine tenor voice. When he spoke his face reflected his deep feelings and love for the unreached Indians of Mexico. In addition, he was good to look at! Hearing him was enough to cause a girl's heart to beat faster, and Marianna was no exception!

At the end of Camp Wycliffe's summer session Bill had returned to Mexico. Marianna and co-worker Evelyn Woodward were assigned to the Chol tribe, also in the state of Chiapas. Leaving her family in Mexico City, Marianna traveled with Evelyn by second-class train, car, horseback, and plane to southernmost Mexico.

Bill Bentley's occasional visits—a long day's hike over the mountains from the German coffee ranch that was his headquarters to the American-owned coffee ranch used as a base by the girls—were warmly welcomed.

On one of his trips Bill brought a large box of cookies made by the German lady at the ranch. In the bottom of the box Marianna found an extralarge heart-shaped cookie meant just for her. It was a sign that love had entered the picture! On a romantic February 14, 1941, the missionary pair pledged to become one, and they decided to be married in the States. Joyfully, Marianna made plans for the wedding. Bill set to work gathering materials for his language informant to build an Indian hut—where they planned to begin their married life.

Bill felt that they should have a small, simple wedding and it was set for Saturday, August 30, in the Slocum home. Rev. Rowan Pearce, head of the Pioneer Mission Agency, was asked to perform the ceremony.

Marianna returned from her first year on the field greatly weakened by amoebic dysentery. Most of her visit at home was spent under treatment by a tropical disease specialist. She and Bill had hoped to sight-see together, but Bill had to do much of it alone.

On Friday, August 22, Marianna felt well enough to drive with Bill to Keswick, New Jersey, where he spoke at an evening meeting. On Saturday they took a train to New York City and spent a happy day hand in hand taking in the sights—Rockfeller Center, the Empire State Building, the Statue of Liberty—there was so much to see and they knew they might not get back again. The train trip back to Philadelphia that evening found them both exhausted, but jubilant in spirit as they looked forward seven days to their wedding.

The next morning Bill was late for breakfast, and Mr. Slocum went to call him. Soon he came back—alone and pale—Bill had died in his sleep and had gone to be with the Lord.

Bill had suffered a serious illness as a child that weakened his heart. Three years of pioneer life in an Indian tribe, going on foot for days over the trails, and fighting off amoeba had further weakened his heart. Bill Bentley laid down his life at twenty-seven before the job among the Tzeltals could be finished.

Marianna's parents promptly contacted Cameron Townsend. At that moment, Marianna remembered something Bill had once written to her: "Since this life is uncertain and one of us may suddenly be taken, leaving the other to continue life's pilgrimage alone, our love must be wholly centered in our Lord himself." Marianna, with courage and God-given consecration, asked to speak to "Uncle Cam." "Let me return to the Tzeltal tribe in Bill's stead; let me finish the work. . . ." Townsend's answer was "Yes."

As the train carrying Marianna, her brother Walter, and Bill's body made its way back to Topeka the following Wednesday evening, she kept thinking of the words Rowan Pearce had said that day. Instead of conducting a marriage ceremony, Rowan had given a memorial message based on John 11:40: "Jesus saith unto her, Said I not unto thee, that, if thou wouldest believe, thou shouldest see the glory of God?"

Over and over the words of Jesus, spoken so long ago to another woman, sounded in Marianna's thinking, ". . . believe and you will see. . . ." With determination, calling upon God for strength, she set her mind for the task ahead.

Bill Bentley was laid to rest in Topeka and Marianna continued on to Camp Wycliffe, arriving Saturday, August 30, the day she and Bill were to have been married. She could not help but remember what had happened just one week before. Had she and Bill really been sightseeing in New York? How could so much have happened in one short week?

She leaned her head back against the seat, closed her eyes and remembered something Samuel Rutherford had written: "He is not lost to you, who is found to Christ." An all-encompassing peace flowed through her tired body as she thought of the words of another, ". . . in his presence is fulness of joy; at his right hand there are pleasures forevermore." Believing this and relying on God, Marianna entered Mexico alone.

Ethel Wallis, another translator, soon joined Marianna and they set out over the trails for the Bachajóns, the lowland group of Tzeltal Indians. There they planned to live in the Indian-style house which Bill had arranged to have built for himself and his new bride. When the two girls entered the area, they were met by hard-drinking, machete-wielding Indians instead of the friendly ones they had left. Confronted with this barrier of hostility, they turned and retraced their steps to the coffee ranch where Bill had lived. There they were given a warm reception and lodging; they stayed in the room which had sheltered Bill.

At the coffee plantation Marianna resumed her studies of the Tzeltal language. Soon she felt the need to move to an all-Indian area, one and a half days' horseback ride from Las Casas in rugged terrain. Through the help of the authorities, she obtained a house where she was able to work with three of the highland Tzeltal dialects. Hour after hour she listened to the conversations of the Indians as they sat on her porch, trying to catch tone inflections, words and phrases.

After a succession of temporary partners, and intervals without a partner, Florence Gerdel, a trained nurse, arrived on January 2, 1947, to help "temporarily." Twenty-one years later they are still co-workers.

The missionaries worked on linguistic and anthropological investigations together, but from the first day Florence had to cope with the connivings of witch doctors and the ravages of alcohol and violence in human bodies. They met hostile stares of dirty, antagonistic Indians and they encountered hindrances from certain authorities. But slowly and patiently the two carried on, making friends and influencing people by their gentle teaching and loving overtures.

Nearly seven years were to pass before anyone from the tribe had the courage to take a stand as the first Christian. All this time Marianna worked on primers in Tzeltal, cultural studies in English, a Tzeltal hymnal and translation of the Gospels.

The shaggy-haired, barefooted, illiterate son of a witchdoctor, Martin Gourd, was one of Marianna's first informants. As he helped translate the Gospel of Mark, he became the first Christian in his tribe. As the first one to believe "the good new words" and to turn away from drunken licentious tribal rites, he had to bear the brunt of opposition from his tribespeople. Undaunted, he carried a phonograph and Gospel records on his back over the mountainous trails to tell others of "the living God in heaven."

In a distant hut, Martin finally found hearts willing to hear about God. The first one to turn to the Lord was Juan Lopez Mucha, who told others until there was a nucleus of eighty

Christian believers in Corralito. Juan amazed Marianna with his spiritual discernment. In time he became one of the leading believers and preachers.

Martin Gourd was to undergo great testing through the years, and yet remain strong and faithful. At one point Martin heard that 140 Indians had set out for his house to kill him; he and his wife kneeled down and prayed. Then Martin got out his records and phonograph and put them in the center of his hut to give the mob a testimony before he died. He waited all day and evening, and no one came near. Truly, God had shielded his own.

While Florence cared for the hundreds of patients who came for medicine, Marianna patiently worked on the translation of the entire New Testament. Persecution of the Indian believers continued, and yet through the years the numbers of Indians attending Sunday service increased. Even during the rainy season, with nearly impassible trails, they came by the hundreds.

Congregations of Christians came into being everywhere as the Word of God was taught. Many learned to read in their own language out of sheer longing to "know what God has said in his Word." Enemies of the Gospel set several chapels on fire; some of the Indian Christians were jailed; one was shot and killed for his faith in Christ. In spite of the opposition the Word of the Lord spread throughout the entire region.

Marianna wrote thrilling letters giving accounts of the amazing things that were happening: ". . . we can only say, 'This is the Lord's doing, and it is marvelous in our eyes.' "

In 1952, when at last a narrow airstrip was leveled near the tribe, Marianna's parents visited her. Her mother had changed from a nominal Christian to a devout, active one, largely through the life and death of Bill Bentley. When Marianna's father saw the hundreds of redeemed and enlightened Indians, he said, with Simeon of old, "Lord, now let thy servant depart in peace, for mine eyes have seen the salvation of the Lord!"

An indigenous church developed among the Tzeltals. Many of the Indian leaders had learned the Word of God as they helped Marianna translate it into their own expressive tongue. They turned to "God's Book" for the solution to every problem in the fast-growing Tzeltal church.

August 6, 1956, the first copies of the New Testament in Oxchuc Tzeltal arrived in the tribe. Indians from many parts of the tribe had gathered at the cornfield airstrip on the side of a mountain. MAF pilot E. W. Hatcher brought the precious cargo in his tiny yellow plane. Over twelve hundred believers streamed to the large, white-washed "templo" for the dedication services.

Senor Francisco Estrello, of the American Bible Society, had made the long trip from Mexico City in order to make the official presentation to the believers. He gave the first copies to Marianna and Florence, and to two translation helpers, Juan and Domingo. For five years these helpers had come at night, after the field work was done, to help "pass God's Word into the real language"—their own tongue.

One of the Indian elders opened the New Testament and read from its pages for the first time in the presence of the whole Tzeltal church: "Blessed is he that readeth and they that hear the words of this (Book), and keep those things which are written therein" (Revelation 1:3).

The entire templo of believers stood to promise before the Lord to "believe, obey, and proclaim" the Word of God. A humble, barefoot Indian elder who had helped translate, quietly stepped forward and prayed: "Lord, it isn't enough that now in our hands we have your Word written in our own language. Write it in our hearts, Lord, and let it be seen—in what we do and say each day—that we believe in you and that we obey your commands."

Hunger plagued the region because of corn scarcity, yet the believers spent their last pesos for a New Testament. Marianna stood aside, trying to keep back the glad tears, watching them with their outstretched hands. It was such a simple act as they reached for and received a copy of the New Testament, yet in that reaching the translated Word of God would "translate" many more into the kingdom of God.

She thought, "They handle their Books as though they had the greatest treasure in the world. Well, they are right, it is; for what else in this world gives the hope of life eternal, the knowledge of sins forgiven, and the power to live a new life triumphant over sin?"

Marianna turned to Florence and said, "Our work here is done. We must move on to those who do not have the Word." For fifteen years there had been an ache in her heart to go back to the lowland Bachajón Tzeltals of the rain forest area who had so viciously rejected them before. She wanted to finish the work begun there by another. . . ."

God wonderfully opened the way. Florence turned over the medical work to the Indians she had trained, and Marianna turned over the teaching of the Word to well-qualified Indian elders. In April 1957, they set off for the unreached Bachajón people. To get there, they flew six minutes in the MAF plane to the nearest town, Ocosingo. Then they walked six hours across a wooded ridge into Bachajón valley, following Indian guides and five pack-animals with their belongings. Four long years were to pass before the Indians would clear a strip in the pine forests for the plane to land nearby.

Again, as they gave God's Word to those who lived in constant fear of death, they saw many quickened to spiritual life. Some who had heard the Gospel seventeen years earlier through Bill Bentley, when they were schoolboys, now turned to the Lord and became leaders of the new congregations forming throughout the Bachajón territory. One of them, Manuel Cruz, became Marianna's translation helper.

In addition to working on New Testament translation—always first and foremost—Marianna was instrumental in preparing Bachajón-dialect primers, a 4,000-word Spanish-Tzeltal dictionary and Old Testament story books. All of these materials would prepare the Indians to be ready readers of the New Testament when it came from the presses.

Word reached the governor of the state of Chiapas that some of the Bachajón Indians, whose reputation for brutality had kept outsiders from entering their territory, were now law-abiding citizens. This he had to see for himself! And so the governor and his party visited the area when an airstrip had been cleared and the MAF pilot could fly them in.

The governor inspected the new school built by the Indian Christians, examined the orderly, well-stocked clinic that ministered to hundreds in the area, and attended an hour-long service in the thatched-roofed chapel. When he left, he was carrying a copy of the Oxchuc Tzeltal New Testament. One of his party departed with a pistol sticking out of one hip pocket and a Tzeltal hymnal out of the other!

And now, once again, another great day came—May 30, 1965—when the Bachajón New Testament, so long in preparation, was to be put into the hands of the Bachajón Tzeltals. Indian Christians from forty-one congregations had come—some of them three days by trail—to be on hand for distribution of the first copies. And the young preacher who had volunteered to carry a box of Testaments from the airstrip to the new, brick chapel was still waiting to hear how much the treasured book cost.

Marianna's throat tightened at the past memories, but she managed to say quite evenly: "Seventeen and a half pesos."

The bearer of the books quickly extracted a hard-earned 20-peso bill (approximately $1.60) from his pocket and gave it to Marianna, and she—with an inexpressible thrill—gave him change.

No, she couldn't relate the years of labor that the Book had cost. Nor the handicap of primitive living conditions, the isolation, illness, unfriendly tribespeople—and the going away of a precious loved one. Besides, he knew all about that. He understood. Hadn't he, too, experienced hardship and persecution? Yes, he and many others.

They reached the chapel. Soon the dedication service began. Domingo Mendez looked out over the hundreds who had gathered. Holding the New Testament in his hands he said, "We have given thanks to God for this Book. Now, are we going to use it? It is not to be put in a box, but used to reach those of our people who do not believe. As you once committed all kinds of sin with your hands and feet, now use your hands and feet in doing what pleases God's heart."

Marianna looked across the crowd of Indians. On hillocks, under every tree and in shady nooks, people were studying, reading, helping others to read and discussing the wonderful truths newly made plain to them. She closed her eyes tight. The tears were close. "Thank you, Lord, for your promise that your Word would not return unto you void!"

Movie cameras were rolling. Strange men and strange-looking equipment had started arriving two days before with the MAF plane. Cornell Capa, *Life* magazine photographer, three crewmen and Hugh Steven, a fellow Wycliffe member, were also present. Senor Daniel Lopez de Lara, representing the American Bible Society, had flown in from Mexico City, to make the official presentation. This was Christian history in the making.

A leading Mexican magazine, *Tiempo,* made Marianna the subject of a 16-column cover story that proclaimed her "the architect of a transformed situation." She had, they declared, lifted an entire Indian nation from barbarism to civilization." The article was titled, "A Woman Brought Them Civilization." (December 9, 1957, issue). *Life's* Latin American edition in Spanish, *Life en Espanol* carried a full report and photographs on August 2, 1965, by renowned photographer Capa describing the Bachajón Tzeltals receiving the New Testaments.

Almost before she knew it, it was departure time for Marianna and her partner, Florence. At least sixty tribes in Colombia, South America, were without God's Word in their dialects. Florence and Marianna looked at each other and linked hands; God was calling them to pioneer a new work there.

Old Chief Marcos Ensin, emotion showing in his wrinkled face and choked voice said, "My children are grown, my family responsibilities are few. I want to go with you to Colombia to tell others to believe God's Word as we Tzeltals have believed it!" But he knew he must leave the task to younger, trained ambassadors. He urged them: "Go, with God, to those without."

Marianna, sitting in the MAF plane, could hold back the tears no longer. She pressed her handkerchief to her eyes. Faces pressed close to the plane window; outstretched hands reached through the open door to touch her once more; others waved from a distance. The warmth and deep love of past years poured forth as they tried to show the women how much they cared.

In the gentle voice which God had used to touch thousands of Indian hearts as she had given out his Word, Marianna said to Florence, "You know, it's much harder leaving than it was beginning." To herself she thought: "Jesus saith . . . if thou wouldst believe, thou shouldest see the glory of God."

The work in the Southern Andes of Colombia began in October, 1964, and continues today. A letter from Marianna about her story concludes with these characteristic words:

"I consider it a great privilege to be among those included in such a book as this.

"The movement of the Spirit of God which resulted in more than one hundred Tzeltal congregations in the tribe, with the New Testament in two dialects, I attribute to two things—Bill's life, which was laid down for the Lord and for the Tzeltals, resulting in a spiritual harvest even as Jesus said in John 12:24, 'Verily, verily, I say unto you, Except a corn of wheat fall into the ground and die, it abideth alone; but if it die, it bringeth forth much fruit,' and my father's prayer life. From the time I left for the mission field in 1940, until he went to be with the Lord himself twenty years later, he lived to pray for me and for the Tzeltals. As he 'stood for the people God-ward' (Exodus 18:19) in a life devoted to prayer, the Lord answered by 'bringing many sons unto glory' from among the Tzeltals.

"May the Lord alone be honored in this book, for we ourselves are only 'unprofitable servants.' 'Not that we are sufficient of ourselves to think anything as of ourselves; but our sufficiency is of God' (II Corinthians 3:5); 'Neither count I my life dear unto myself, so that I might finish my course with joy, and the ministry which I have received of the Lord Jesus, to testify the gospel of the grace of God' (Acts 20:24)."

Cameo eight

Traveling on

Millie Dienert

What compels a woman who loves her home and family to travel alone across 27,000 miles of ocean and continents to unknown places? What impels her to rent a car at the end of that strenuous journey and drive through Southern California's "impossible" traffic to another engagement?

Business? Adventure? Duty? Emergency? Yes, and no.

The real answer is many-sided, yet amazingly simple. It's many-sided because there are many facets to the character and story of Millie Dienert. Her much-traveled childhood years, her troubled teens, the trauma of a broken engagement later followed by a wonderful marriage, and busy, exciting events since then make up the dark and sparkling facets of her life. The simplicity of the answer lies in the singleness of direction Millie has traveled since she yielded control of her life to God.

For Millie, finding that answer wasn't simple at all. It took many years—and many failures. Running away from God, rebellion, pride, a stubborn will, assertion of self, these and other attitudes took Millie on aimless detours until certain extremities of life closed in. It was as though a large stop sign rose up before her, and human extremity becomes God's opportunity.

Millie's rebellion against God began in the pent-up emotions and special restrictions that come to a minister's daughter. She was born Mildred Elsner in Brooklyn and raised in Greater Manhattan. Her parents traveled endlessly in evangelistic work, and this only child was partially reared by her grandmother. When Dr. Theodore Elsner settled down with his wife and daughter, it was to become founder and pastor of Calvary Memorial Church in Philadelphia. Theirs was a very devout home, but Millie Elsner didn't always appreciate that.

Psychologists would call what happened to this child a direct result of her feelings of resentment and insecurity, for Millie in grades one through four was considered a hopeless stutterer. She says, "I will never forget the kindness of the teacher who tutored me. At one point she put her arms around me and said, 'Mildred, we're going to lick this and you'll be amazed at what's going to happen to you!' " It was licked, and not only Millie but many others as well have been amazed at what has happened to her, for today Millie Elsner Dienert is called by Billy Graham "the world's most dynamic woman speaker."

In the big downtown church which her father pastored, Millie often had occasion to hear the preaching of the famous Gypsy Smith, Billy Sunday and other noted evangelists. The church was widely known as a center of constant evangelistic activity, and the preaching of outstanding men of God had an irresistible effect on her life.

Millie participated in the youth activities of the church, but inwardly the feeling of rebellion was growing. Dreams of a professional dramatic career took firmer shape as she enrolled in the Emily Kreider Norris School of Expression. Long before this, the stuttering of her childhood had left. With a natural flair for the dramatic, the training was a delight. At the same time, she also enrolled in the Philadelphia Bible Institute. It was an attempt, perhaps, to apply a salve to her conscience, that wee, small voice which would not let her go her own way.

During Millie's teen-age days, she was in an automobile accident which snuffed out the lives of several companions. She was so shaken by the experience that she came to a full stop in her dash toward personal freedom.

As she floundered for answers, the things she'd been hearing from her parents, church leaders and the great preachers began to merge into a serious question: "Why did the Lord take my friends and spare me?"

Conflicting questions came as she hesitated on the edge of a life-changing decision: "Do I want to 'regress' (as she regarded it) and go back to my childhood training?" But then, the choice made, Millie prayed, "All right, Lord, here's my life. . . ."

And yet there were reservations in her heart, Millie now realizes. She says, "It was as though I said to God, 'You can have my life, but give me myself.' "

An emotional extremity arose in a marriage engagement that was broken. The sorrow taught Millie that God is very near the Christian, and that he becomes more precious to the lonely soul that leans on him.

About a hundred young people comprised the backbone of the Calvary Memorial Church. Among them was a fellow named Jim Truxton who later was to found the organization, Missionary Aviation Fellowship. Another was Walter Smythe, who would become co-ordinator for the Billy Graham Crusades. A third was a lanky six-footer named Fred Dienert.

Fred was converted through the preaching of Millie's father, and he became a member of the Board of Directors for the youth work at Calvary Memorial. Millie was strongly attracted to his relaxed personality—and thus began a romantic involvement.

In 1938 Dr. Elsner conducted the marriage ceremony which made Millie Elsner and Fred Dienert man and wife. Dr. Elsner and his wife watched through tear-brimmed eyes as their daughter took this joyful step. For them it meant answered prayer and a son-in-law of whom they were proud.

Through subsequent years the Dienerts experienced the usual problems and joys of parenthood. Theirs has been a full life complicated by the fact that Fred Dienert travels almost constantly as an executive in the Walter F. Bennett Advertising Agency. Early in her formative years, Millie had told God she'd never live with a man who traveled. As she reflects upon her marriage, it is with a sense of God's greatness for he took away this feeling and replaced it with the willingness to be both mother and father to their three children when her husband is away.

Millie admits there have been moments, particularly when

her son at the age of fourteen became desperately ill, that she felt the numbing sense of fear. But God always proved faithful and mastered her fear. At such times Millie experienced a sense of Jesus' presence similar to that of his disciples when he appeared in their midst and said, "Peace."

During the summer of 1950, through an unusual chain of events, Dr. Elsner met Billy Graham and urged him to go on radio. Elsner told Billy of his son-in-law, whose partner, Walter Bennett, had promoted and handled many national religious programs.

Shortly after that, when Billy Graham began a six weeks' crusade in Portland, Oregon, Bennett and Dienert urged the evangelist to go on the air waves. Billy was not easily convinced, knowing it would be very costly and time-consuming. But true to his calling, Billy poured out his heart in prayer about the matter. In answer to that prayer, God provided exactly the amount of money Billy needed and had asked for. That was the beginning of the worldwide radio broadcast heard each week known as the *Hour of Decision.* This was Fred and Millie Dienert's introduction to the work of Billy Graham. Little did they or Billy realize what the future held in store for all of them.

In December, 1955, Millie was involved in another car accident which nearly cost her life. This led to deeper introspection . as she realized anew the unique and precious privilege of knowing the One who performs miracles! She suffered head injuries which caused intense suffering and "retro-active shock." Physical complications developed and discouraging diagnoses were given, including permanent impairment to eyesight and retentive memory problems—"but God intervened."

Anyone who has heard Millie Dienert speak will affirm that the power of God's healing is evident in her life.

If Millie experienced misgivings about the extent of her husband's travels taking him away from her and the children, she was to undergo the same qualms about her own itinerary. In spite of her desires to be a "homebody," her appointments seemed to snowball.

In February of 1966, she was asked by Graham Crusade

directors Walter Smythe and Bill Brown to come to England to assist in the Prayer Preparation Program which precedes all crusades. Jean Rees, wife of Mr. Tom Rees, and Millie met women in various churches. There were never less than 200 women present, and sometimes as many as 900. Encouragingly, some were converts from a previous Graham Crusade. Of this experience Millie says:

"We saw nothing less than the power of God as women rededicated their lives and, motivated by the Spirit, offered to open their homes for prayer in their communities. (This seems to be an unusual thing for British women to do). At the end of three weeks I returned home. Then from the middle of May until the first of July we were in London again for the Crusade. During this time, women's coffees, luncheons, and teas were called in many areas of Greater London as another arm of evangelistic outreach."

Whenever possible, Millie's youngest daughter accompanied her on extended trips. By 1966, her oldest daughter was married and her son away in college.

In June 1967, the Dienerts went to London again to participate in the All-Britain Crusade. Twenty-five cities viewed the meetings on closed-circuit TV, another milestone in the outreach of the Team. In the fall of 1967, Millie journeyed to Tokyo, Japan, where she again assisted in the Outreach operations and spoke at women's meetings.

Another facet in the Millie Dienert story was etched "against the grain." She tells it like this: "In 1958, the National Christian Women's Club sent an area representative to Jenkintown, Pennsylvania, where we lived. I was not at all anxious to get involved in one more thing; I decided this was not for me and tried to forget it.

"But then I began to see the Lord work through this local Club, not only reaching unconverted women, but also helping the Christian women whom I knew. I saw their spiritual vision broaden. The Spirit of God spoke to me through II Samuel 24:24. It was five o'clock in the morning, and I shall never forget it. The words remained to convict me: 'Neither will I offer burnt offerings unto the Lord my God of that which doth cost me nothing. . . .'

"After that I asked again for the leading of the Lord. He prepared my heart and I learned that my involvement was his will. Christian Women's Club work has given me a new vision of the role of women. I had felt I had a broad vision as far as the work of women was concerned, and I couldn't see interchurch groups working harmoniously together. Narrow-mindedness, bigotry, this was all I could imagine.

"The reservations I'd had were dissolved. I began to view the work of Christian Women's Clubs and Councils as a part of the highway-and-hedge call to which our Lord referred. The intent, vision and purpose of this work is to introduce women to a vital personal relationship with Christ. There are now more than 550 clubs across the country, and work has also begun in Canada and other foreign countries. Headquarters is at Stonecroft in Kansas City, Missouri. Every time I go there and walk on the grounds I feel I am treading on holy soil. I was drawn to the ministry because they are dedicated to prayer."

Millie has served as local chairman for two years, area representative two years, and now is a National Consultant for the organization. In this capacity she makes frequent cross-country trips speaking to Clubs and Councils. It is a work of love, her answer to the bidding of the Holy Spirit. Her expenses are never underwritten, and organization speakers go to great personal effort to keep such commitments. Surely II Samuel 24:24 has taken on real meaning for this seemingly inexhaustible woman.

A close observer of human nature, Millie Dienert has come to recognize the efforts of CWC speakers as a seed-sowing ministry. She says, "One of my most interesting experiences had its beginning in suburban Washington, D.C., where I was speaking to a Christian Women's Club luncheon group. Concluding the message, I saw no visible response. At such times one is inclined to feel a little disappointed.

"Years later I was speaking for a Palos Verdes Club in California. A woman came up afterwards, her eyes swimming with tears and said, 'I've been meaning to write to you for four years. I made a decision at a luncheon in Washington, D.C., when you spoke, and since then my husband and four children have come to know Christ in the same way.'

"Once again I realized the results of our seed sowing is between God and the individual. If we sow in faith diligently, God will perform miracles. As in nature, the sower sows and the right climatic conditions bring forth the flowers and fruit, and those conditions are in the hands of the Creator, not ours."

The Dienerts have a thirty-nine-year-old business in which Millie participates. It was purchased in 1955 and the original name retained: Farenwald's. It is located in "An Original Farmhouse of Jenkinstown, Pennsylvania." (The community is now called Jenkintown.) Specializing in flowers, decorating and imported gifts, the shop attracts a select clientele from suburban Philadelphia.

In addition to her interest in this business, Millie conducts Bible study groups in suburban Philadelphia and adjacent New Jersey communities. She believes such groups are a return to the days of the Acts of the Apostles when the Word of God was being shared in the homes.

As Millie Dienert travels around the world, she sees God on the move, not only through such men as Billy Graham, but through homemakers and business women as well. Her message, as God has given it to her, is that Christians everywhere must see that one person plus God is a majority, and that God does his work through those who are willing to be channels of his purpose. Personal evangelism must be the work of all Christians.

Millie observes: "Our churches are packed, but I am not impressed. We barely have our feet wet spiritually. We just barely know what it is to be a child of God."

At the time this was written, Millie was in the midst of a weekend conference involving over 600 women. She had traveled more than 27,000 miles in the previous six weeks. The last lap of that journey had seen her in a dash from the Los Angeles International Airport in a rental car through heavy weekend traffic over unfamiliar freeways to Forest Home Christian Conference Center in the San Bernardino mountains east of Redlands. No southern Californian would get on a freeway at five o'clock on Friday evening if he could possibly help it. Only the homeward-bound and beach- mountain- and desert-bound vacationers are willing to endure the nerve-wracking, bumper-to-bumper traffic. But even though it was new to Millie, she came out on top.

When she arose to speak, she was refreshed—and refreshing! Her first sentences conveyed the vitality of God's grace in her life. She was returning from Australia and New Zealand where she had participated in the prayer programs for a forthcoming Billy Graham Crusade. Her travels had taken her into little, old Scottish towns, across the bush country of Australia where kangaroos, snakes, birds and wildlife are plenteous, and back into the great cities. At one point she went without sleep to arrive in Brisbane just in time to speak to 2,000 women.

Wherever she goes, her encouragement is the same: "Not all of us have dramatic experiences in life; not all of us are called upon to travel to the far corners of the world; but all of us can experience the same, exciting infilling of the wonderful Holy Spirit."

Thus, compelled by the love of Christ, Millie travels and travels, somewhat as her father once did, knowing now that obedience to God always brings the Christian to the right destination.

Cameo nine

Poor Little Rich Girl

Charlyne E. Haden

Looking back over the years I can see that a definite struggle has long characterized my life. It was the struggle of a child's tender soul trying not to lose its bearings in a confusing, cruel, capricious world. Mine is the story of disillusionment, of pain and hurt. It is the story of a prodigal who wandered—and came back home.

I grew up in a troubled family. Few realize the depths of the scars inflicted on children when the two people they love most are at war with each other. And like other children reared in a similar situation, I early learned the habit of worrying. I worried my childhood away. The past disturbed me; the future frightened me. And since I was so obsessed with what had already taken place and what might take place, I didn't think much about what *was* taking place. The present didn't concern me. I was waiting—for what I didn't know. In a way, like Sleeping Beauty, I was waiting for life to begin.

Yet as I look back on my childhood, I realize that the Lord actually blessed me by this affliction. It created in me a peculiar need. And out of this need, I became very religious. Religious in that I sought above all else to reach heaven. I tried to be honest, honorable, and trustworthy. My Bible, Sunday school, and church partially satisfied my inner longings. Yet I was not a Christian, as I did not know Jesus Christ as my Lord and Savior.

My mother wanted her children to attend Sunday school and church. My father had no faith. He had left the church years earlier. Father was a very successful man. He gave us the world as he knew it; he could not give us the Lord whom he did not know.

I suppose my family had more cocktail parties, did more traveling, saw more horse shows, and lived socially higher than anyone else in our town. Our family was spoiled and indulged, but not one of us was truly happy.

As the years passed I became a restless soul—seeking, asking and looking for I knew not what. I attended a different college each year. I showed an unusual aptitude in art; but even that didn't mean much to me. I loved college, did well, but was soon bored. Nothing held my interest for very long.

By the time I reached adulthood I lived in a world of "greys." Everyone I knew seemed to live in this same world. No one went to church—that had long been the thing not to do. This grey world—in a way—was a very pleasant world in which to live. Black was not black—nor was white, white. I did not demand too much from myself, and I demanded even less from others. I considered myself a very broadminded person: tolerant, understanding, compassionate. Oh, I had many faults and weaknesses, but I was *tolerant.* It never occurred to me that this "grey world" had few standards and principles. Everything seemed relative to the situation at hand. The religious nature I had cultivated as a child soon was glossed over with a heavy coating of sophistication. But deep underneath a childish soul was seeking someone to listen and to answer.

Upon graduating from Finch Junior College in New York City, I took a year's course in interior decoration at the New York School of Interior Design. I later became a high fashion model for Conover in New York City. As a fashion model I appeared in *Harper's Bazaar, Vogue,* and *Glamour* magazines. I guess I wanted to model to prove that I wasn't as ugly on the outside as I felt on the inside; for by this time, I was beginning to have a very guilty conscience. At first modeling was thrilling; but within a few months, like everything else I tried, it became a bore.

I was seeking a new world, but unfortunately I sought it in

the same old world I had always known. I went the way of the world—and I was miserable. Guilt weighed heavily on my shoulders. I longed to be a child again—to be untarnished, to be clean. But there was no way out. The world was all around me, and I had no place else to go.

Some years after these deep doubts began, I married Ben Haden, a Virginian, after knowing him for about two months. We met over a bridge table on a Sunday afternoon. You might call it love at first sight, but before the year was over it was a different story. In the words of my husband: "Our marriage wasn't quite bad enough for a divorce—and certainly not good enough for a marriage."

One night in 1952, while living in Washington, D.C., we decided to go hear Billy Graham. Ben said he was bound to be a great entertainer. I went out of curiosity—I came away a new person!

It was a most unforgettable evening. I've never attended anything like it before or since. I remember marveling at the mink coats present; I had expected to see just the "well scrubbed" look. But then the music began, and it changed into a sacred, inspiring service. When Billy Graham gave an invitation to publicly confess faith in Christ, I was frozen to my seat. Could I really be clean again, clean as a little child? Could all my sins be washed away by the blood of Christ? Suddenly I knew that more than anything in life I wanted this new life in Christ.

We were seated in the top row of the highest balcony—and I was very shy. But on Billy Graham's last invitation he said, "You come. You come, there in the balcony! You come. He'll wait for you. He'll wait for you!" I was the last one to walk forward that evening. The platform seemed miles away, but I could not stay in my seat. My husband was horrified! He tried to pull me back into my seat, but I had decided to go. Ben followed me down the steps—simply to avoid losing me in the crowd!

I walked alone with the Lord that year. And yet I was never lonely. I didn't know one other Christian. In fact, it was several years before I did. I seldom went to church, but when I did my soul was not fed. But the Lord blessed me with a great desire to read the Bible. And he gave me the greatest peace of heart I'd ever known. The old restlessness slipped away like a shadow in the night! What I had sought so hungrily as a child—and longed for as the years passed—had come at last. And life really did begin for me.

We moved to my hometown of Kingsport, Tennessee. Ben became busy with the work he loved—newspapers. He was vice-president and general manager of the daily and Sunday newspapers. Ben was president of various civic clubs and was all-out for the town. I was busy with Junior League, art classes, bridge parties, and the Cerebral Palsy Center. It was during this time that Ben accepted the Lord in a men's Sunday school class taught by Sam Anderson, a layman.

We taught a joint Sunday school class of seventh- and eighth-graders. We thought we were contributing, but our lives seemed more dissatisfying each year. We were still going the rounds of the cocktail circuit and mingling with the country club set, but more and more often we would be dressed for a dance or a party only to pay off the babysitter and stay home instead. Our activities seemed pointless. The reason is obvious now, but at the time it wasn't. Now we realize that we were not doing what the Lord wanted us to do with our lives.

The Lord blessed us with a daughter, Dallas, after six years of marriage and several miscarriages. God has peculiarly protected this child. Twice in the middle of the night he awakened me with a start to send me dashing to the nursery where I found that the pacifier which Dallas was never without had come apart and she was on the verge of swallowing it.

Another time I very foolishly left our three-year-old Dallas and my sister's six-year-old Rhue in the car while I ran to do an errand. I took the keys, put on the emergency brake, locked the car, crossed the parking lot and climbed two steep flights of steps. Then I heard someone yelling and saw him pointing toward my car! Dallas was at the wheel, pretending to drive—and laughing her head off. The car was moving straight toward the edge of the cliff. I shall never forget the hopeless horror I felt as I ran for the car—knowing that if I caught up with it I would not have time to unlock the door! I can still see little Rhue frantically trying to roll down her window. The

Lord stopped that car just short of the cliff. Workmen nearby watched in awe.

The changes were many as we realized our lives had to be different. Our marriage began to be a most wonderful companionship. We learned that when a couple has the Lord in common they have the most important thing of all. Today—frankly—I think it is extremely difficult for any marriage to succeed without Christ's help. There are never enough hours in any day for my husband and me to share together. We talk into the wee hours each night; we have a fellowship I never dreamed possible. The Lord took a marriage that was nothing and made it into something very special!

And the Lord showed me, a reserved, introverted person who had sought confidence and self-improvement in every course that crossed my path—from the DuBarry Success Course and Dale Carnegie Course to the latest speedwriting course—that he and he alone is the true source of confidence. He gave me a confidence that I had never been able to attain. A person must like himself in order to be confident, and before Christ came into my life I didn't like myself at all.

Shortly after my husband's conversion he thought the Lord wanted him to go into the Christian ministry. But neither he nor I had the least desire to do so. It took a trip to the Soviet Union to show Ben that the claims of Christ mean everything to a man—or nothing. This fact had never dawned on us.

With many misgivings—but with genuine peace—we left Tennessee for seminary training. We went from a world of "beautiful people" and beautiful things to what was to us a most austere world. Seminary time was the most difficult three years of our lives. The economic adjustments were tremendous, but the spiritual battles were even more overwhelming.

I had thought the years at seminary would be the most spiritual years of our lives. Instead, we found we had to fight inner battles to keep our faith every hour of the day. Our experience was that seminary is where some of the front-line fighting is done for the Lord Jesus Christ. Ben was already an attorney; but he found seminary more difficult than law school. On top of all the rigorous schooling, the daily trial of personal faith was almost too much. But the Lord saw us through—and he has repaid time and again for all those things we gave up.

Mark 10:29-30 became the verses I lived by: "And Jesus answered and said, Verily I say unto you, there is no man that has left house, or brethren, or sisters, or father, or mother, or wife, or children, or land, for my sake, and the gospel's, but he shall receive an hundredfold now in this time, houses, and brethren, and sisters, and mothers, and children, and lands, with persecutions: and in the world to come—eternal life."

Upon leaving Columbia Seminary in 1963, we took our first pastorate in Miami, Florida, at the Key Biscayne Presbyterian Church. It was a small church which we dearly loved. It had a warmth and zeal for the Lord that was inspiring. While in Miami—and on Dallas' ninth birthday—we adopted a second daughter, Leigh. Later, in October, 1967, the Lord called us to the First Presbyterian Church in Chattanooga, Tennessee. We are beginning to feel very much at home in Chattanooga— needed and loved. I think I will be content to spend the rest of my days right here among these dear people in this fantastically beautiful city.

In February 1967, the Lord opened for Ben a most wonderful opportunity. He was chosen to be the speaker on The Bible Study Hour—the worldwide ministry begun many years ago by the late Dr. Donald Grey Barnhouse. Ben can be heard on many stations throughout the world on Sunday mornings. Our prayer is that the Lord will continue to prosper this ministry.

The radio program has put us somewhat in the limelight, bringing blessings as well as problems. The mail is voluminous, and there are never enough hours to answer all of it! The demands on Ben have naturally increased, but the Lord gives us strength day by day. All the extra effort and frantic rush of additional responsibility become as nothing in comparison with the opportunity! As we work on radio messages together, our life purpose remains the same: to introduce unbelieving, empty lives like ours once were to the quiet confidence and joy and power of knowing Jesus Christ.

And to think—all this is ours and heaven too!

Cameo ten

Partners Together With Him

Marj Saint Van Der Puy

"It is one thing for two people to fall in love and get married, but quite another thing for eight people to fall in love and all 'get married.' " So says Mrs. Abe Van Der Puy, the former Marj Saint, widow of jungle pilot Nate Saint, missionary martyr to the Auca Indians of Ecuador.

When Abe Van Der Puy, president of the World Radio Missionary Fellowship with headquarters at station HCJB in Quito, Ecuador, became a widower in 1965, the difficulties and adjustments to make with three motherless children loomed large.

Marj Saint was no stranger to the situation in which Abe found himself. From personal experience she knew the problems, loneliness, and needs facing Abe.

On January 8, 1956, as Nate Saint and Pete Fleming prepared to leave Shell Mara for Auca territory to accompany Jim Elliot, Ed McCully and Roger Youderian to the river clearing they had named Palm Beach, they had reminded Marj and the other wives, "Pray for us . . . today is the day things will happen."

That day went down in church history as the day when five courageous, talented young men paid the supreme price to "preach the gospel to every creature." A waiting world heard the sorrowful news, as did the five composed wives. The magnitude of the events of that day and the fruit of the martyrdom have since been seen and felt in lives around the world.

For five women, the day signaled the advent of widowhood. For their children it meant no father. But their faith was stronger than fear, and the song which the men had sung the morning they left became the refrain the widowed women took up as they faithfully carried on:

We rest on thee, our Shield and our Defender,
We go not forth alone against the foe.
Strong in thy Strength, safe in thy keeping tender,
We rest on thee, and in thy name we go.

We go in faith, our own great weakness feeling,
And needing more each day thy grace to know,
Yet from our hearts a song of triumph pealing,
We rest on thee, and in thy name we go.

There were to be many moments, many days, through the long years ahead when Marj Saint would look back and recall with thankfulness the words of that song.

It was Abe Van Der Puy who, as an HCJB staff member, received the news of a plane crash in December 1948, which involved Nate. Nate and Marj had been in Ecuador only three months then. Abe brought the word of the mishap to Marj and took her to see Nate in the hospital. It was Abe and his wife, Dolores, who were instrumental in seeing that Nate received proper medical treatment.

It was Abe who, when the five fellows were reported missing in Auca territory, came to Shell Mera, the Missionary Aviation Fellowship base where Marj and Nate lived, to report the latest information to HCJB and by shortwave to the world.

Again, it was Abe who wrote the condensation of the book *Through Gates of Splendor* (which tells in detail what happened those fateful days) for *Readers Digest* in 1956. And Abe was the one decorated by the Ecuadorian government, as the missionary representing the men who gave their lives to contact the remote jungle tribe.

Following Nate's death, Marj and the children—Kathy, then seven, Steve, five, and Phil, one—moved from the jungle to Quito. Abe Van Der Puy was field director of station HCJB, and so Marj's direction in her new missionary work came from Abe.

Through subsequent years the Van Der Puys and Saints were neighbors, and the six children of the two families were the best of friends, especially Joel and Steve—now sixteen years old. The missionary community and the radio audience, as well as the Van Der Puy family, lost a beloved friend when Dolores Van Der Puy died.

Marj continues the story: "Even before Abe mentioned to me his intention that someday we should marry, his three children told him they wanted another mother now that the Lord had taken Dee, and 'Aunt Marj Saint' was their choice. Several years before the marriage, my daughter Kathy had requested I include Abe's name on our will as one who would be responsible for her, Steve and Phil in case of my death, 'because,' she said, 'I think he is the nicest older man here.' Steve had told me he never wanted me to remarry, that he, Kathy and Phil would take care of me. But when Steve knew 'Uncle Abe' wanted to marry me that was fine!"

Thus it was that on a beautiful August day in 1966 eight people who had come to love each other dearly became a family. Abe and Marj chose to have the wedding performed on the HCJB missionary compound grounds. A lovely Ecuadorian home had been offered them for the happy occasion, but choosing to include all their co-workers, the national Christians, and a host of friends and well-wishers as guests, it was decided that the ceremony should take place at HCJB. Dr. Reuben Larson and Senor Enrique Romero officiated, over 800 attended and the children took part in the wedding ceremony.

A pictorial record of the wedding and a brief letter followed shortly thereafter to friends and relatives around the globe. Of the wedding they said, "There's not much to write this time. The pictures tell the story. Many wonderful friends helped and attended, making the ceremony on August 25 something we will always remember with great joy. We've had a delightful time together as a family—all eight of us. . . . We desire that the

Lord will use our lives and our home for his honor. Solemn responsibilities and great opportunities face us in gospel service here at HCJB." The letter was signed, "Happy as can be, Abe and Marj."

Marj continues their story: "Phil, who had never known what it meant to have a father in our home (as he was only one when Nate died), was always coming up with comments that warmed our hearts. One day after we were married, Abe was helping Phil repair his slingshot. I walked through the room where they were working and Phil smiled at me and said, 'Boy, life sure is different for me now.' I replied, 'It surely is for me, too, Phil.' He grinned and said, 'Well, not nearly so different as it is for me.' Little did he know what it meant to me to not only have Abe's love and attention for myself, but to see the children thriving on it after ten years without it. Just the other day Abe and Phil were together somewhere and out of a clear sky Phil told Abe, 'I love you so much that I can't even seem to remember when you weren't my daddy.'

"For several months after our marriage Abe and I would count our blessings and say, 'It is just too good to be true.' Then we decided that wasn't a very Christian way to express our true gratitude for what the Lord had done in giving us each other, so we've changed it to, 'It is so good it must be true.' "

Part of their honeymoon was a trip to the First World Congress on Evangelism held in Berlin in October 1967. There they had the heartwarming experience of seeing the Auca killers of the five missionaries giving their testimony as to what it now meant to know and love Christ. Rachel Saint, Nate's sister, was there with them. Together Rachel, Marj and Abe rejoiced in God's goodness.

Marj's letters are a glowing tribute to her newfound happiness as wife of the man charged with increasing responsibilities as president of the World Radio Missionary Fellowship. Of this new role she says, "I am a nurse, but with my new responsibilities that come with being married to the one in charge here, I found it wasn't feasible to work in our mission hospital, so am helping with the work in our mission accounting office. I'm finding it much easier to leave a typewriter and numbers than to leave medicines and patients on a moment's notice. We find also that one of our responsibilities and pleasures in this official capacity is hospitality. We feel that our children are very privileged to get to know those who love and serve the Lord."

The Apostle Paul, in writing to the Christians in Rome, reminded them that they were to be "given to hospitality." One senses, in reviewing the life of Marj Saint, as she lived it on the MAF Shell Mera base with Nate (so beautifully told in the book *Jungle Pilot*), and in her capacity as hostess in Quito that here is exemplified the "hospitality" which Paul exhorted.

A typical day described by Marj reads like this. "I had just started this note and a missionary couple came by. They needed help in getting a muscle biopsy packaged and off to the States. Their daughter here is very ill. By the time we got it ready, it was lunch time, so I asked them to stay. Turned out there were four of them, not two, and Abe had just called to ask if another missionary friend could come. So at 11:55 we changed the table from five to ten and ten shared the food cooked for five. I just didn't offer seconds, nor did I offer apologies. We had a wonderful time of Christian fellowship."

Abe's work includes missions to the United States, Europe and Panama. This puts the Van Der Puys in touch with many people constantly. Of this Marj says, "In spite of the many pressures of work in these days, we have so much for which to be thankful. The Lord had given us good friends in the U.S. who continue to support us even though neither of us has spent much time there in the past twenty years to renew and maintain the usual type of friendships, and our responsibilities are such that we even often neglect our correspondence.

"We try to write a weekly carbon copy letter to the three children in the States and our four sets of parents and in-laws (which include Nate's and Dee's parents). We are convinced it is important not to let work completely push out the time we need to spend with the boys here at home, but we are also convinced that quality is more important than quantity, and feel the Lord has given us a wonderful relationship with them.

"We make ourselves available to talk to the children about the joy or problem of the moment, even if they find it necessary to come to the offices where we are working, or awaken us when they come home at night. We've had good times playing tennis and fishing with them, or eating lunch at 10,000 feet on the mountain behind our house. But I think we would all agree that the most precious moments have been during the hour at suppertime when we talk about the happenings of the day and then together read an article, a chapter of a book, or a portion of Scripture. It is a very informal time, and even a magazine article has often prompted a good, healthy discussion on practical Christianity."

If Marj writes glowingly of her happiness as Mrs. Abe Van Der Puy, she is doubly happy mothering six children. "Abe's three children, at the time of this writing, are Lois, now twenty-three, Mark, nineteen, and Joel, sixteen. Mark and Joel were both born in Ecuador. Lois is now working in Chicago waiting for an assignment with the U.S. diplomatic service. She is musically like her mother. Mark attends Tennessee Temple College and has a basketball scholarship which helps pay his expenses. Joel is in high school and is also very athletic. He and Steve are on the basketball team and are both mountain climbers, having climbed several of the snow-covered peaks here in Ecuador, one which took them to 19,300 feet.

"My children are growing, too. Kathy, nineteen, attends North Park College in Chicago in the school of nursing; Steve, sixteen, is in high school at the Alliance Academy in Quito. He is a good student and active in everything including all sports. He shows a keen interest in business, mechanics and aviation. Phil, thirteen, also attends the Alliance Academy. He doesn't excel in school work, but does well with anything mechanical, especially planes. Twelve years ago Nate described them as Kathy the go-getter, Steve the diplomat, and Phil the persuader. It still holds true today."

Marj is frequently called upon to visit and counsel with those who have experienced heartbreak or tragedy, or are undergoing sorrow. Out of the depths of her past experience she draws the needed strength to assist those who are looking for help and guidance. Of these times she says, "What a spiritual experience it is to see God do for others what He did for me those many years ago."

She also conducts a weekly Bible class for the American

Colony women, does her weekly marketing with another HCJB wife, manages to play tennis once a week, shares a radio program with Abe each week, goes with Abe to conduct listener follow-up in other parts of South America when able, and always is ready, with Abe, to answer the children's questions about everything from studies to girls.

As Marj looks back, she can, in all sincerity, say that the years since Nate's death have been a resplendent blend of varied experiences, all the work of the Master Weaver.

Following the Palm Beach martyrdom, Marj came to the United States and shared the story of her and Nate's life and what had transpired in Ecuador. As she spoke to various groups, she used this poem which so vividly portrayed her feelings:

The Weaver

My life is but a weaving
    Between my Lord and me,
I cannot choose the colors
    He worketh steadily.

Ofttimes he weaveth sorrow,
    And I in foolish pride
Forget he sees the upper
    And I, the underside.

Not till the loom is silent
    And the shuttles cease to fly
Shall God unroll the canvas
    And explain the reason why.

The dark threads are as needful
    In the Weaver's skillful hand
As the threads of gold and silver
    In the pattern he has planned.

—Author Unknown

In September 1961 Marj sent a copy of a letter to the States which her son Steve, then ten, had sent to her from Aucaland. He was there six weeks. The letter, with spelling here just as he sent it, went like this:

Dear Mom, Kathy, & Phil,

I am having a very nice time. The first days I was hear they killed two taypers. So they had enufe to seat and smock. I went on a fiew fishing trips with the indiens and Sammy. ·One time we got quite a few fish. I always have fun because everytime they catch a fish they say ta, ta, ta, ta which means I got it and you can't get it away from me. When we heard that we all speared at it. A couple times I got it.

I got a parot the other day from Anty Rachel. A couple days after I got the parot he rebelled against me. He was on a balsa log which rolled. The parot got scard and hopped over on me and he slipped and got mad at me so he pe, pe, pecked meee, mee, me three times, but at least I have something to write about. Oh by the way, his or her name is Pollyanna. Right know he, I mean she is on Mingcayes roof doing knothing.

For the last few days the Aucas have been trying to catch a teagrillo that has killed about 20 chickens. The other night he went right in the Kechua boy's house to get a chicken. The man heared him and yelled because it was dark and he couldn't find his gun. But his yelling scared it away.

The same boy made Sammy and I a canoua. If I sit in it, it will tip, but we ly in it and the water pushes us. But when we are in a place where the water doesn't push you, you have to paddle with your hands. The other day the boys saw a dear and everybody chast it. Dayuma had a fishing spear and when she tried to spear it, the fishing spear brock so she allways keeps her spear handy. The jock about it is that the ladys aren't supose to spear things so they got some fun out of that.

Mom, I know about 20 words of Auca now.

By for know your beloved

Saint Steven

by

Marj had added: "Well, so much for that. I do hope
his spelling improves in the next few years. Ha, ha. I
do think this was a wonderful experience and am
grateful to Rachel for taking him home with her...."

Rachel Saint has made her home with the Aucas since 1958.
Through the Auca woman, Dayuma, who served as informant,
Rachel was able to live among the savage Aucas and learn their
language and culture, and to show them the love of Jesus which
miraculously changed their lives. This was told in the books
The Savage My Kinsman and *The Dayuma Story,* and in
various publications that have reported the developments in this
amazing story.

In July 1962, Kathy Saint, then thirteen, spent a month in
Aucaland with her beloved Auntie Rachel. Her letter reveals
that there was no fear nor hatred harbored by the Saint children
and their mother toward those who had killed their father and
husband. The letter read as follows:

"...I'm sitting in the school room, and Auca 'sala'
(living room) of Aunt Rachel's house, and I have
quite a view. Kimo and Dawa are in their house
chewing monkey meat. Dewey is making darts. Uba
is trying on a pair of nylon leatards, and Gikita is
practicing with a new spear he made for one of the
pilots. After supper we have 'Auca night school' so I
help teach them to read and write (at the same time I
learn more Auca words). About 18 Aucas have taken
their first step toward Christ and out of them nine
have been baptized."

Perhaps the most amazing part of the Saint-Van Der Puy
story occurred in 1965, which Marj shared in the following
letter.

"The children and I recently had such an unusual
experience that I want to tell you about it. We went
with Rachel, Dayuma and ten other Aucas down to
'Palm Beach.'

"Palm Beach is still the little paradise the five
fellows described it to be ... and there are still as
many bugs. We saw the spot where they built the
small shelter, the area where they tried to show the
Aucas by signs how to clear a landing area in their
village, and the place where the destroyed plane stood

before the swift waters washed it downstream. We swam and fished in the river right where the five fellows swam and fished and enjoyed their hydraulic siestas. We tried to imagine how it all seemed to them almost ten years ago.... We sensed no uneasiness or fear, and I doubt they did either. Then we walked back through the trees to the place where the rescue party had buried our men.... And the Aucas pointed out to us the stump of the tree that had served for the tree house. If there were any possible way to describe to you that which was in my mind and heart ... I would gladly share it ... but there seeems to me no way for one to tell another ... I felt as Ken Gosney expressed in prayer as we stood there in the jungle, 'Lord, our words and emotions are all backed up.'

"The baptismal was the highlight of our trip. Some months before, Kathy had written from school in Florida saying she would like to be baptized this summer and thought the perfect place would be Aucaland during her visit with Aunt Rachel. Then a friend suggested that Palm Beach would be even more ideal ... and I'm sure it was. The service was simple ... Dayuma read for all to hear from the Gospel of Mark recently translated into the Auca language. Then Dyuwi sang the Auca equivalent of 'Jesus Loves Me.' Four were baptized, my Kathy and Steve, Iniwa, Dayuma's adopted brother, and Oncayi, the downriver Auca girl who joined this group about a year ago. Kimu talked so seriously to each of the four explaining that when one is baptized, he is saying to all that he truly loves the Lord and wants to walk pleasing to him. When they were again back on the beach, Kimu prayed a very long prayer speaking to God about each one of us individually. My heart was touched even more when he recognized before the Lord the difference in their two trips to Palm Beach. He said, 'Father, when we came here a long time ago, we did a bad thing when we killed those foreigners, but today we have done what we know you wanted us to do and some day all of us will meet in the air to go to be with you.' Rachel interpreted for us as he prayed. I truly wish each of you might have been with us and seen and heard all this with your own eyes and ears."

Many years went by in which Abe Van Der Puy had no opportunity to have a direct part in the Auca work, though much was happening. Then in late 1967, Rachel Saint wrote to Marj and Abe, inviting them to the Auca Village of Tiwaeno and asking that Abe baptize a group of Aucas who had trusted Christ as their Savior. Abe and Marj wanted to go right then, but it was impossible with the work load in Quito, and the months rolled by.

In February of 1968, however, Dr. and Mrs. Marshall Daniels from Rockford, Illinois, special representatives of HCJB, came to Quito. Marj and Abe made arrangements to go with them to visit the jungle base of Wycliffe Bible Translators, thinking that while there they could get over to Rachel and include the baptism. Marj relates the incident.

"The Lord had another plan. We were happily surprised to find Rachel, Kimo and Oncaye (Auca Christians) there. That night Rachel asked Abe to accompany her, the Auca girl Oncaye, and Don Smith, the Wycliffe pilot, on a flight the next day over the downriver Aucas who had not yet been reached with the gospel. They took off early the next morning and flew directly to the area in the jungle and then circled low over the houses for almost two hours. Don Smith, the pilot, circled over the clearing deep in the Ecuadorian jungles. Oncaye, on some low passes, was sure she saw some of her family. Oncaye then called to the Indians on the ground through a loud speaker on the wing of the plane.

"Oncaye spent time identifying herself, finally convincing them she was the one who several years before had fled in fear from them, and now she knew about God and wanted to be with them again. Thus convinced, twelve of the downriver group Aucas met Oncaye and others from the Tiwaeno Aucas on the trail on February 15, and came back home with them. Oncaye's mother and two brothers were among the group. Many have prayed for this contact for eight or nine years. We are grateful to God for seeing his plan fulfilled."

God's plans are not thwarted. We see this in the events in Marj Saint Van Der Puy's life since that day in January, 1956, when Nate said, "Pray for us ... today is the day things will happen."

Nate, in his letters home, had written of his capable wife, saying, "Marj still keeps everything in order and in hand. Everyone asks how she does it. I don't know either. The Lord surely knew that in this kind of work I would need a partner with a brain like a filing cabinet and one incapable of saying 'can't.' "

At one point, when Marj was stricken with appendicitis, Nate had said to Ed McCully, "Pray for Marj. If anything happened to her I wouldn't be worth anything." And in the book *Jungle Pilot* we read of Nate referring to Marj as "my six-armed wife."

But Marj and Abe have counted on the reality of Jeremiah 33:3 to accomplish their tasks: "Call upon me, and I will answer thee, and shew thee great and mighty things, which thou knowest not."

And so, together, they call upon God in their appointed place at HCJB in Quito, Ecuador, where the Voice of the Andes is faithfully "Heralding Christ Jesus' Blessings." Jesus said, "In the mouth of two or three witnesses every word may be established"—and these "partners together with him" (Zachariah 4:6) give convincing testimony that "the Word of the Lord is sure."

Cameo eleven

Led Home
By a Daughter

Thelma Elfstrom

Even a first glance at Thelma Elfstrom reveals matured and refined womanhood. To know her, however, is to know someone who has gone through the crucible of deepest testing and has emerged with refinement of which the Psalmist speaks: "For he holds our lives in his hands! And he holds our feet to the path! You have purified us with fire, O Lord, like silver in a crucible" (Psalm 66:9-10, *Living Psalms and Proverbs*).

The silvery-haired newspaper publisher's wife had everything a woman could possibly desire. Her eminently successful husband provided her with a lovely home, beautiful clothes, furs, cars, opportunities to travel widely and shared with her the joys of three beautiful daughters.

Of herself Thelma says, "I prided myself on knowing only the 'best' people and moving in their circles. I was an egotistical snob! But when our precious daughter lay dying from aplastic anemia, after having been given a potent antibiotic for a minor infection, we had no possession whatever that could be used to save her life. We could have flown doctors from anywhere in this world, but it wouldn't have helped."

Nineteen-year-old Brenda Elfstrom, youngest daughter of the Edgar Elfstroms, attending a university thirty miles from her home, awakened in the early morning hours with a throat so sore she could not swallow her own saliva without great pain.

Her housemother immediately contacted Brenda's parents.

When the phone rang at three o'clock that May morning in 1960, Thelma Elfstrom could not imagine the nightmare of anguish that would stalk their happy family for the next three weeks. Nor could she perceive that in God's divine plan both she and her husband would come to know—through this heartbreaking experience—that they could not run their own lives. God does hold our lives in his hands, and our feet to the path. He it is who purifies us with the fire of personal suffering, and brings us through, to present us, like silver in a crucible, before his Son.

Thelma tells the story like this: "We brought Brenda home, and at daylight took her to the hospital. Through the help of a doctor neighbor and friend, we were put in touch with a fine internist. I sat beside my suffering daughter while the doctor made a small incision in her chest (he was testing her bone marrow). It seemed but minutes later that he called me out of the room. He laid a trembling hand across my shoulder and made the awful pronouncement that there was virtually no hope! My husband's first words were, 'If there is even a small chance, we are going to fight. What can we do? Where can we get help?'

"We secured the services of one of the most able hematologists on the West Coast. He used every skill, every means at his disposal, but in three dreadful weeks our dear one was gone.

"Those were three weeks of excruciating suffering for Brenda. I stood by her bed, hour after hour, applying iced cloths to ease the high fever and pain that racked her body. I watched in agony as she almost left this world that first week as her blood slowly hemorrhaged away. I watched as the doctor gave her that first blood transfusion which gave her miraculous new life for a few hours. I applied medication. I think I died a little with her.

"As those last hours of life on this earth were drawing to a close for Brenda, she asked me to read the Bible to her constantly. I held her hand and read to her by the hour. Many times she seemed unconscious and I would quietly ask if she would like for me to stop. She would always answer, 'No, Mamma, it helps me.'

"The presence of God was very real in that hospital room. I

pleaded with him to spare my child, but the time came when I knew he was going to take her home. I held her fevered head tight in my arms and looked up to him and said, 'All right, Father, I accept your will. I give her back to you. Just tell me what you want me to do and help me to bear it.'

"Although I did not realize it at the time, God literally enfolded me in his wonderful grace. For many weeks the only feeling I had in my heart was one of love. There was no bitterness. I had been through God's fire of judgment, and my soul and my spirit emerged from the dross cleansed and chastened.

"During the next long months I tried to find meaning and purpose in life. Activities and pleasures that had so engrossed my time and attention all the years before were now meaningless. There *had to be* something better.

"About this time it was necessary for me to undergo major surgery. During my convalescence I was more and more aware of an inward need to read the Bible. God had really indicted me when my daughter had asked me to read the Bible to her. I realized then, with heartsick dismay, that I didn't know where to look to find the comforting words she needed. But folded in the pages of the Bible I had hastily snatched from the library at home, I found a list written in Sunday school by Brenda's sister, Diane, of proper biblical references for 'trouble,' 'sickness,' 'death,' etc. God in his mercy had provided!

"We had always considered ourselves a Christian family. We went to church on Sunday; we saw to it that our daughters attended Sunday school regularly; but Jesus Christ and the Bible had no real place in our lives. We prayed to him when we wanted something, but we didn't really want him to intrude. We were doing just fine running our own lives—or so we thought."

While convalescing from surgery, shortly after Brenda's death, Thelma made up her mind that the very first time she was able to leave the house she would go to the public library to find books that would help her understand the Bible. She did just that, coming home with two books, the Old and New Testaments in story form.

"As I read once more the heartbreaking torture of our Lord as he hung in agony on the cross I broke into uncontrollable tears. For the first time his wonderful love became real to me. I also came to the full realization that Jesus Christ had died on that cross for me! He was offering me a new way of life, one of peace and quiet joy—eternal life!

"The next day a Christian friend whom I knew only slightly came to call. We spent the entire afternoon talking. I told her of Brenda and how God had revealed himself to me during and after those tragic days. She invited me to a Bible class that met every Tuesday. I readily accepted. From that day my spiritual eyes began to open.

"This friend and her husband invited us to visit their church—a sincere Bible-teaching church. Our lives began to change, to take on new meaning. In 2 Corinthians 5:17 we read, 'Therefore if any man be in Christ, he is a new creature: old things are passed away; behold, all things are become new.' This is the miracle that took place in our lives.

"As my husband has grown in faith he has found many ways in which our newspaper (*The Fullerton Daily News Tribune,* Fullerton, California) can be used for Christ. A daily column by Dr. Billy Graham is widely read by thousands of subscribers. New opportunities appear constantly where the pages of the newspaper can be used for our Lord.

"When Brenda died my husband dedicated himself to do something about the indiscriminate use of the potent antibiotic that had caused her death. We had learned from experts that Brenda's minor infection did not justify the use of this particular drug. We also learned from newspaper friends around the nation who volunteered to help my husband that many others had suffered and died similarly." But before Edgar and Thelma Elfstrom launched into their crusade to stop the indiscriminate use of this powerful drug, they spent long hours in prayer seeking God's guidance.

In their investigations Thelma and Ed Elfstrom slowly amassed a mountain of shameful evidence concerning the thoughtless use of this drug. They gave freely of their money and their time—putting in countless hours of work that carried great heartache and traveling numerous miles. The president of the United Press International came to their aid by offering them the vast facilities of his organization. Eminent doctors were interviewed and gave much help. Twice during the first two years after Brenda's death the Elfstroms flew to Washington, D.C., to sit in on the drug hearings of prominent legislators and to interview Food and Drug officials.

At one point in his search Mr. Elfstrom, along with a group of newspaper publishers from across the country, was invited to the White House for lunch with President Kennedy. When Mr. Elfstrom was introduced to the President, he immediately said, "Oh yes, I've heard about you. Keep up your good work"—and he indicated his appreciation and approval of the cause.

Today the Elfstroms have the satisfaction of knowing that their determined relentless efforts have curtailed the misuse of this drug. Medical journals now print warnings on its use and danger. And scores of letters from all over the world assure them that many lives have been saved because of their concern.

Thelma now explains their tragedy and subsequent work this way:

"From the standpoint of the world Brenda's lovely young life was used so that others might live. We believe it was God's plan. He has given us two other dear daughters. God knew the misuse of this dangerous antibiotic was causing untold deaths of which the world, including much of the medical world, was unaware. He knew my husband was a strong and determined man. And most of all, God knew that of all our family, Brenda loved him the most, and her short earthly life reflected it. We believe that his work in her, on earth, was finished.

"Many friends have said, 'Thelma, how can you not be bitter? You and Ed were good parents and you loved your daughters. How can you love a God that does this to you?'

"My answer is very simple. I do not believe God makes mistakes, and I do not think he made one in our case. God is holy, loving and compassionate; he is a God of justice. At no time did he promise me that I would have my children with me all of my life.

"I do not look upon death as punishment. The Bible is full of wonderful assurances of the beauty, peace and wonder of heaven. In the book of Revelation, the great Apostle John, inspired by God wrote, 'And God shall wipe away all tears from their eyes, and there shall be no more death, neither sorrow nor crying, neither shall there be any more pain; for the former things are passed away.' Then, in I Corinthians we read, 'Eye hath not seen, nor the ear heard; neither hath it entered into the heart of man, the (wonderful) things which the Lord hath prepared for them that love Him.' I believe these things from God's Word, and it gives me the peace I need to accept what has happened.

"As I look about me at the things that are happening in the world today—the breakdown of moral standards, of loss of self-respect, the frustrations, the growing evil—how could I wish to bring my dear one back to this? Yes, very often I long with a mother's heart—that never really forgets—just to hold her close once more. But God promises in his Word that one day we shall be reunited, if I am faithful. I rest on his promises.

"This was the divine and infallible judgment of God. We can accept this. God 'invaded' our lives, as it were, through this experience; but, we can only praise and thank him for it!"

Once she restlessly sought the transient activities that glorified herself. Now, with a sense of walking in the right direction, Thelma Elfstrom seeks above all else to glorify Christ. From dark doubts, questioning, crying out and fighting, she has moved into the sunlight of peace and quiet joy as she has surrendered to God's Holy Spirit. She rests secure in a world of growing insecurity. She has gradually turned from a life of meaningless searching to one that is filled with purpose. She spends much time reading and studying the Bible, and in intercessory prayer. She participates in Bible study classes and frequently speaks to Christian Women's Clubs. She is concerned to speak and help, in the name of Christ, whenever and wherever she can.

The Elfstroms feel that their experience with God has been one of continual gain. Not only has God taken nothing material away, but the more they try to give to him, the more abundantly he replaces it. God changed their point of view and put emphasis on the spiritual or real values of life, providing guidance and direction in the use of things and material resources. He has held their lives in his hands, and their feet to his path and brought them to himself. And for anyone who will pray, as Thelma Elfstrom did—"Father, I accept your will . . . tell me what you want me to do"—he will gladly hold them in his hands. He eagerly helps those who unequivocally accept his ways.

Cameo twelve

Madam Navigator

Lila Trotman

Skipping along on her way home from school, nine-year old Lila Clayton was merrily minding her own business. Down the street roared an old "Model T" Ford, throttle wide open, driven by a teen-ager who sat on the back of the seat and drove with his feet! His companions roared with laughter when he took a huge, very ripe watermelon, and threw it at the unsuspecting Lila. It landed at her feet, completely splattering her.

Terrified, she ran home, screaming and crying. Lila Clayton's mother quickly looked at her frightened daughter, thought she was covered with blood and dashed to call her husband home from work. By the time Lila's father arrived home, Lila had managed between sobs to tell her mother it wasn't blood, but watermelon!

When William K. Clayton learned what had happened, he was fit to be tied. Grabbing up his daughter, watermelon mess notwithstanding, he put her in the car and off they went, looking for the "yardbird," as Mr. Clayton called him! To this day, Lila Clayton Trotman is certain her father would have killed Dawson Trotman—yes, the guilty party—if he had found him. But God had a plan for Dawson's life *and* Lila's.

Can you possibly imagine Mr. Clayton's reaction, some years later, when he found out who the fellow was who had thrown the watermelon? The "yardbird" became William Clayton's son-in-law! Though Lila Clayton regarded Dawson Trotman's actions as "mean" that day, in later years she came to regard that episode as a teen-age prank quite typical of Dawson's before-Christ days. The Dawson Trotman she came to know, admire, *and* love was as different from that young prankster as night is from day.

Lila Clayton was born in Buffalo Valley, Tennessee, the second of six children into a home filled with love; later, the family moved to Lomita, California, near Los Angeles. In the same little town lived Dawson Trotman. Though frail physically, and slight in stature, young Trotman excelled in schoolwork. He had a remarkable ability to make and keep friends and was elected student body president in his senior year of high school. This ability to win the cooperation of others, God used in later years after Christ became a living reality in Dawson's life.

When Lila was thirteen Dawson had been a Christian about sixteen months. He threw himself into the young people's work at the small community church and became an ardent witness for Christ. He had a deep concern for the young people with whom he came in contact. One young girl particularly caught his eye, and he asked her, "Are you a Christian?"

"I've gone to church all my life," was her confident answer.

Dawson looked kindly at her, but said sternly, "I didn't say, 'Are you a churchian?' but 'Are you a Christian?' "

"I've been baptized," she replied, somewhat less confident.

Not satisfied, he kept on, "But are you a Christian?"

"Then I don't know what a Christian is," she confessed.

This conversation was characteristic of Dawson's dealings with people—understanding, patient, persistent. That day he explained to Lila Clayton the simple gospel story, and how she might receive Christ into her heart and have eternal life.

When Lila returned home she was greatly troubled with the realization that she had never asked Christ into her heart. After several sleepless hours of tossing and turning, she got up at two o'clock, knelt down beside her bed, and invited Jesus Christ to be her Savior.

Already a mature young lady at age thirteen, she looked and acted older. Dawson Trotman kept a watchful eye on Lila Clayton for more than one reason!

Dawson was twenty-one and all out for Christ. Scripture memorization had been the key to his conversion, and he knew, as he progressed in his young Christian life, that such memorization was giving him an insatiable hunger for more of what God had to offer. It was a great joy for him to lead someone to Christ. And when he did, he immediately challenged the person to memorize Scripture—just as he had done and was doing. Then he would show them how they could establish a daily prayer life and keep in fellowship with the Lord. Lila Clayton was no exception. Even though she was young, she accepted Dawson's challenge—and her life was transformed.

Dawson started her on Proverbs: a chapter a day to be read and a verse a day to memorize. She responded readily to this personal discipline which Dawson practiced and taught. He had learned that every new-born babe in Christ needs follow-through help from more mature Christians; and so, from time to time, he carefully examined Lila's progress in her Christian walk.

Dawson's love for Christ and his concern for people led him into activities in which he could tell others about Christ and help them live the Christian life. His first Sunday school class grew from 6 to 225 boys who had accepted the Lord. He had prayed, "Lord, you made little boys. Give me an idea how to win them for You."

By this time he had begun to attend the Bible Institute of Los Angeles and was also assisting in the local Fishermen's Club, a gathering of men whose object was to learn how to win people to Christ through individual witness.

But, busy as he was, Dawson took the time to pursue what was turning out to be a warm friendship with Lila. Lila, in turn, had come to admire and respect the energetic and devoted young man who had led her to Christ. Even though he was eight years older, when he asked her to "go steady" her heart hammered hard responding, "Oh, yes," and somehow she managed an audible reply.

God's Word was always foremost in Daws' thinking and he saturated himself with it: memorizing a verse a day, studying it, reading it, and praying over it. About this time he asked a friend to join him in asking God to do some great things, claiming the expansive promises of Jeremiah 33:3 and Ephesians 3:20:

"Call unto me, and I will answer thee, and show thee great and mighty things, which thou knowest not."

"Now unto him that is able to do exceeding abundantly above all that we ask or think, according to the power that worketh in us."

Rising early, following Jesus' example, the two friends met in the hills at five every morning to pray. They prayed for two hours before reporting to work! They prayed for the boys in the Bible Club by name and for nearby towns from which requests had come for help with boys; then, they began praying for cities up and down the California coast. God enlarged their vision and they began to ask him to use them and other young fellows in each of the forty-eight states; and before long, with a map of the world spread out before them, they were praying for the world.

Of those days Lila says, "Rarely ever, during our nearly five years of courtship, did we take a day for ourselves. Daws was hard on himself, and therefore, on others. To him, God required *our very best*; and, I'm sure, during those years, I was, by far his toughest 'trainee.' But, he loved me *and* cared; and too, wanted me to learn early how to walk and talk with God."

It was during this time that God gave Dawson the idea which led to the organization of a group known as the Minute Men, out of which later grew The Navigators. Aim of the group was "To know Christ and to make Him known." To accomplish this, however, Dawson labored unceasingly—dreaming, planning and working out new methods and means. Billy Graham has stated, "He seemed to have a sanctified imagination that could look beyond handicaps, circumstances and barriers. He planned big things for Christ. . . ."

Regarding Dawson's vision Lila comments, "God built into Daws' life an unshakable faith 'that, what He had promised, He was able also to perform.' My own faith grew as I watched the Lord answer Dawson's prayers. Our children often mention their gratefulness for a father who taught them to look to the Lord in confidence for the little things as well as the big."

Saturated with God's Word, and humbly obedient, the

Minute Men diligently set to work promising God they would touch one life daily for him. In later years Dawson was to refer to this as spiritual reproduction. His own spiritual discipline was spreading to others. It was a contagion of multiplication based on 2 Timothy 2:2 which Dawson felt to be Paul's method of training Timothy in the work of the Lord, and meant to be followed: "And the things that *thou* hast heard of *me* among many witnesses, the same commit thou to *faithful men*, who shall be able to teach *others also*." This remains today as the keynote of Navigator work.

Lila Clayton was eighteen when she became Dawson's wife. Though young in years, she had a spiritual maturity that Daws recognized would make her a fitting teammate. He was very much in love with Lila, and she shared the same depth of feeling. "My life had been totally made over by the Holy Spirit since my conversion five years before. I was completely in love with Dawson, but had much to learn to be a helpmate to him. I'm grateful it was a step at a time, a day at a time, and that Dawson was so loving and patient. I am the richer, by far, for knowing and living with this man of God. I fell short in being *all* the Word teaches we are to be as wives—helpmates. But it was wonderful trying!"

There are many who would dispute Lila's estimation of herself. Addie Rosenbaum, who was Dawson's secretary for eleven years, has this to say about her: "Daws was ever seeking to help us grow (in the things of the Lord). He had a way of asking the thing that demanded courage, trust or special willingness, and then of not settling for a half-hearted response. Lila shone at these times! The most outstanding characteristic about her was the way she so willingly and lovingly shared of herself and all she possessed, including her beloved Daws, with the many of us who, through the years, have been a part of the Nav family."

To both Lila and Dawson, the Lord and his work were always first, their partner second by deliberate choice. They took Isaiah 60:11, "... thy gates shall be open continually; they shall not be shut day nor night," as the motto for their home. They were married on a Sunday and opened their home on Wednesday. Living in San Pedro, California, gave them tremendous opportunities to bring sailors home. And so, a steady stream of navy men came into contact with the Trotmans. It was Dawson's firm conviction, shared by his wife, that one of the greatest soul-saving stations in the world is the home.

At first they lived in a tiny room in an auto court. To earn their livelihood Dawson worked at a small service station. Lila cheerfully prepared meals and served them to the sailors at the service station. As one sailor after another came, Dawson and Lila introduced them to Christ, speaking with such love and conviction, that the men clearly saw and eagerly accepted what God so freely offered. Dawson and Lila were thrilled and thankful as they saw these navy fellows developing what they called "spiritual sea legs." Then, whenever these sailors were in port and had leave, they found their way back to the Trotman home where Lila and Dawson guided them into Bible study and memorization of scripture, guiding them carefully toward Christian maturity.

When there was evidence of real growth Dawson would challenge the men in turn to be "spiritual reproducers," and the sailors would go back to their ships and shore stations. Thus was born the name "Navigators" as the influence of these navy men began to spread. The name has remained to this very day, and is now known world-wide.

Lila's warm hospitality, her ability to adapt to all kinds of situations, provided the perfect home situation. Joyce Enright, a nurse who was to come into the Trotmans' life in later years (and care for Lila during illness), has beautifully described this gift of Lila's—that of sharing herself, her home, husband and family with others. "I arrived at Glen Eyrie (the Nav headquarters purchased in 1953) as a trainee. I was awe-struck, especially by Dawson Trotman's wife. Upon my arrival I was told by Dawson that I would be staying in their home and would use my nursing experience to help Lila who was in bed with tuberculosis.

"I was frightened at the very thought of meeting her and much more frightened at the thought of living in her home! How quickly she put me at ease. And how readily she shared her life and her home with me. I was soon to find this was not unusual. She has freely shared her heart and life—good and bad—ever since. This always costs the individual much, I have since discovered.

"I feel Lila 'counted the cost' early in her Christian life, and knew when she married Dawson that he was an 'all the way' Christian. She has never turned back or regretted her decision to likewise 'take up her cross *daily* and follow Christ.' "

Soon after the auto-court days they moved to South Pasadena, California, to larger quarters where the servicemen and others could come. From that time on the Trotman home was the "Navigator Home," a center of operations for this unique ministry which began to spread to main cities in the United States. Even today, the mention of 509 Monterey Road conjures up wonderful memories for the many who crossed the threshhold of that home.

One such individual was Betty Greene who had just received her discharge from the WASPS (Women's Air Force Service Pilot). Miss Greene came to the West Coast to open an office for a fledgling organization later to become known around the world as MAF (Missionary Aviation Fellowship).* When the Trotmans learned of Betty Greene's need for an office, Dawson immediately offered space in the Nav headquarters, which by then was in downtown Los Angeles.

But, Betty not only needed office space, she also needed a place to live—and in the latter part of November, 1944, she moved into the Trotman Nav home, living there for almost a year. Her recollections of life in their home are vivid. "Several things stand out in my mind as being particularly amazing about Lila—her complete faithfulness to Daws in the true sense of the word, a helpmate which showed itself in everything she did in caring for him and their children; and then the way her heart expanded to include so many others. This evidenced itself in the practical ways that go into being a good wife and mother. The home life for everyone was lived like clockwork. It had to be with so many involved, but it was lived with warmth and a deep feeling of love. Almost always there were fifteen to twenty people at the table.

"Lila had some assistance, one of the girls at that time was

*See the Betty Truxton story elsewhere in this book

LaRue Bogue (who later became the wife of Charlie Riggs who is now a Billy Graham Team member). But even so, the responsibilities which fell on Lila's shoulders were tremendous and she saw to it that everything ran so beautifully.

"Daws insisted that if anyone in the household had a complaint against another, they go to the one involved and talk about it, not discussing it with others. This sound biblical principle, true to Daws' and Lila's beliefs, was strictly observed and one of the keys that contributed, I believe, to the harmony in the home. They were very much in the Word at all times, and drew upon it in regard to everything. For me, it was a practical demonstration of abiding in Christ at all times."

Lila herself explains those early formative years. "The Navigators really started in April, 1933. We lived at headquarters and had others living with us. Dawson brought kids from various parts of the United States so we made a home away from home for them. It was a rich, rewarding experience for us. We never had less than twelve around our table, and usually sixteen to eighteen. We have precious ones serving Christ in various places around the world with whom we were privileged to work and live.

"Often I wonder where I would be today if I had not been taught how to memorize the Word of God, how to know 'This is the way, walk ye in it. . .' It is pure joy living with the One who truly has been my Husbandman, my Comfort, my Shield, my Provider, my Joy, my Breath—the Lover of my soul. Eternity won't be long enough to praise him for *all* he is to me, has done for me, given to me—my beloved Dawson, precious children and grandchildren, and friends around the world. We are all 'heirs together of the grace of life' (I Peter 3:7)."

Together Daws and Lila read and studied the Bible and books telling of the lives of such outstanding men of God as J. Hudson Taylor and George Muller. They were deeply challenged by the great faith of these men; and, following their example, trusted God for daily provision for their large "family."

One day Daws came to Lila and said, "Lila, God has so blessed this work! Do you realize that men from every one of the forty-eight states have been reached for Christ? God has answered those prayers we prayed years ago in the early morning hours."

When World War II ended, many of the servicemen, as they returned to civilian life, came to Dawson for counsel as to how they might best serve the Lord. Today those men are serving Christ in mission fields around the world as well as in the United States. Thus God answered Dawson's prayers that the world would hear about Christ.

Dawson produced a Scripture Memory course and devised materials for personal Bible study.** Requests for this material were snowballing. Churches and groups were also requesting trained men to direct them in using the material. Navigator homes which had, up to this time, largely been a shore haven for sailors on liberty, now became places for rallies, civilian Bible study groups, and the planning of area conferences.

On March 1, 1948, Dawson embarked for the Orient. Preceding this he and Lila had a few days' retreat in the mountains with Rev. David Morken and his wife where Dave had laid before Dawson the great need for Daws to move out with the Navigator work "to the uttermost parts of the world." Dawson had said to his wife, "Lila, I know Dave is going to ask me to go to China. What do you think?"

With unwavering faith Lila had answered, "If God leads you to go, go." In her heart she knew this would mean separation from the one she loved so deeply; she knew the burden of caring for the five children would be hers alone. But she knew also that God had a prior claim upon her husband's life and that she must not stand in His way.

This was no small matter. By this time the Trotmans knew for a certainty that their youngest son, Charles, would forever be an invalid. Lila, with great tenderness, tells of this. "I know the heartache and heartbreak, and long, long hours and nights of caring for a precious one who didn't even know who his Daddy or Mother was. I must confess that I have gone through great anguish with his constant crying, but always I was assured and re-assured by my dear Lord Jesus, 'Be not afraid, Lila, I am here with you.' I know God could have healed him, and our little daughter Faith prayed often for our 'Chuckie.' Those were

---

**Available at local Christian bookstores; or write The Navigators, Colorado Springs, Colorado

precious prayers asking God to make her little brother well so he could laugh and play. Then later, she asked that Chuckie could be well so he could have a nickel or a dime to spend, or, so he could run, sit up and talk. BUT, *our God,* the ONE Who CAN do anything, had other plans. I know He will share them with me when I see Him face to face, and until then, I'm reminded of the song, *God Leads His Dear Children Along,* and I am content to be so led."

Though this was a crushing experience for Lila and Dawson, they recognized God's hand at work—a molding and shaping of their lives—so that they could better identify with others undergoing severe trials and heartache. They claimed Psalm 115:3: "But our God is in the heavens: He hath done whatsoever He hath pleased." They cared for this son in their home for eight years before placing him in a hospital in 1953. He was taken home to heaven in January, 1959.

At the time of their marriage Lila's father did not know the Lord, and her mother lacked assurance of salvation. God, in his all-knowing way, used two of the Trotman children to reach these grandparents for himself. Daws enjoyed telling about this: "When Ruthie was three and Bruce five they went to visit Grandpa and Grandma. Grandpa tried to get them to repeat nursery rhymes. He asked for *Mary Had a Little Lamb* and *Little Boy Blue,* but the children asked, 'Who is Little Boy Blue?'

"Their mother said, 'Why don't you quote some of your Bible verses for Grandpa?' This they did, first John 3:16, then Romans 3:23 and others. This delighted Grandpa. He took them all over showing everyone how well the children knew the Scriptures. In the meantime the Word of God was doing its work. It was not long before the Holy Spirit, through the voices of babes, planted the seed in the grandparents' hearts. 'Out of the mouth of babes and sucklings hast thou ordained strength. . .' (Psalm 8:2)."

Addie Rosenbaum, as Dawson's secretary, was especially close to the work in those years. She recalls, "Whenever Dawson went on a trip, Lila planned for all of us to be at a farewell meal and then at the train or plane. And then, his coming home was an important occasion when we all went along to share in the excitement. Lila unselfishly wanted to share these times with us.

"Her interest in the total Nav ministry never seemed to flag. Each evening as we left the office it was my responsibility to take a folder to her. It contained most of the day's correspondence to and from Dawson and other items of interest to her. This seemed to be a daily highlight for her.

"Daws and Lila were an outstanding example to all of us as they learned of Chuckie's illness and went about to adjust to what was probably one of the most difficult things ever accepted by them from the hand of their loving God. Never did I hear either of them question or complain about it.

"There were times when Lila's health was not the best. I know how much she has suffered physically herself, as well as with others of us as we have gone through one crisis or another. I remember her at the foot of *my* bed as the nurse prepared to wheel me off to surgery, and then waking up to find her there when things were all over. Her parents were so dear to her, and she took our parents to her heart as well. So, when it wasn't possible for my mother to be there, she seemed to feel it a privilege to stand in for her, no doubt at some sacrifice to herself. She did this for others also. I esteem Lila most highly and thank the Lord for the many ways my life has been enriched by her."

The work overseas was expanding at a rapid rate. Lila's first trip abroad was in 1950. Then in 1954, she accompanied Daws to the Greater London Crusade at Harringay Arena. This was a memorable time as together they had the privilege of working with the Billy Graham Team in the training of laymen and women for follow-up work. Billy Graham and his Team still use the program that was designed by Dawson Trotman at the evangelist's request.

It is quite widely felt that one of Dawson Trotman's greatest ventures of faith occurred in 1953, three years before his death. Because the Navigator work had expanded so greatly a large central headquarters became a dire necessity. In a most miraculous way God provided the means whereby a 1,013 acre estate known as Glen Eyrie in Colorado could become the property of The Navigators. It was God's provision, in answer to prayer, as a training base for men and women who could then go out into the world, knowing Christ, and making him known to others.

Not long after making the move to the Glen, Lila was confined to bed with tuberculosis just after having had back surgery. She had been in bed for five weeks, and then again underwent another major surgery. About these difficult weeks she says: "Daws had to move out of our bedroom, the children couldn't come into my room, and our beloved crew could only talk to me through the windows. But, those months in bed were very rich ones. They gave more time to pray, to read, to study and write letters. Then, as the doctor lifted the ban I had many wonderful hours with scores of visitors."

In the booklet *The Pathfinder*,* Lorne Sanny has described what happened in early summer, 1956. "On the afternoon of June 18, 1956, ten people who were attending a Christian conference in upstate New York were speeding in a power boat across Schroon Lake. Suddenly a wave struck the boat, hurling two of its occupants into the water. The man held the young girl's head above the water while the boat circled back to them. Just as she was lifted to safety, her rescuer sank beneath the waters and disappeared from sight.

"The man who thus died saving the life of a girl whose name he did not know was Dawson E. Trotman, founder and director of The Navigators. . . ."

Widowed, and with four fatherless children looking to her for guidance and strength, Lila Trotman courageously moved forward. Joyce Marston (now Mrs. Don Enright), the nurse who lived with the Trotmans and cared for Lila during her illnesses, remembers the days following Dawson's homegoing very well. "Outstanding to me—even more now that I am married—is Lila's reaction over months and years to the death of her beloved Dawson. As can be imagined this changed her life more than it would for some women. She was no longer the wife of the president.

"Many bear up in public, in those first days and weeks, but later question God's ways. Not so Lila. I was with her almost constantly for weeks and months after Dawson was taken, and

---

*Available at local Christian bookstores; or write to: The Navigators, Colorado Springs, Colorado.

often went with her when she just wanted to get away.

"God was *truly* her sustenance, her comfort, her all. And her faith in his perfect ways—as learned from Dawson for so many years—saw her through unique adjustments.

"Lila is also characterized by not being a 'respector of person.' I have seen her as deeply concerned about 'little people' (in the world's eyes), as she is about those who are well known, have wealth, or are in some way the kind of person most of us tend to cater to. She is genuine in her interest in and concern for each individual and has shown it in many ways.

"She has been known to buy a suit for a trainee or staff member about to be married, when she learned he didn't have one. She will sit and listen or talk to someone whom she has just met at the sacrifice of her own schedule. Her words of encouragement, and her faithfulness in correspondence, especially to those overseas, cannot possibly be measured or counted.

"Sensitivity to the needs of people was typical of Dawson, causing them both to become involved in the lives of others without thought of what it might cost them personally—an involvement that is rarely seen. Their tender concern God has used to reach men and women as they have found Lila and Dawson's approach hard to resist.

"Lila also has the wonderful ability to laugh. She is one who has learned that God meant for us to enjoy life. Again, one could not live in their home and not know they enjoyed living and had lots of fun.

"Top this all off with her unassuming, humble spirit—and a desire, above all else, to please and glorify God. I know her weaknesses, but they are overshadowed by her life's desire that everyone with whom she comes in contact should know her God. Therefore, I can say in getting to know Lila so well, I have gotten to know her Lord. In her case, one cannot separate the two."

Betty Skinner, at Navigator headquarters, close to the work and Lila writes, "Outstanding about Lila is her genuine love and dedication to serving those of her Navigator family, her specific interest in the welfare of each one, and the positive influence of her life in so many practical ways. She has a strong, daily walk with God that enables her to accept with patience both the expected and unexpected. A strong thread through her life is that of Psalm 115:3 (quoted earlier), the deep-dyed conviction that God is in charge.

"Much of Lila's time since Dawson's death is given to traveling for Nav. Her administrative role in The Navigators is as a member of the Board of Directors. She speaks to women's groups around the country, and is a special blessing to small groups of Navigator collegians and others who come to Glen Eyrie, sharing just from her life and experience with the Lord."

Following Dawson's death, in September of 1956, Billy Graham invited Lila to join them in working with the Team for the New York Crusade in 1957. Since then she has had the privilege of being with them in many other Crusades. Billy and Ruth Graham have maintained close contact with Lila Trotman through the years, and shown great tenderness and concern for her welfare.

Lorne Sanny, as President of The Navigators since Dawson's death, speaks with deep-felt respect and love of his memories of Dawson and the influence of Lila in their lives. "I once asked my wife Lucy where she learned to work so hard. 'From Lila,' she answered. It was my privilege to live in Daws and Lila Trotman's home for some years and it was a rich experience. The close and constant association of living and working with Daws was, I believe, what God used to train and prepare me for the responsibilities I later was given. And of course, Lila along with Daws had a vital part in our lives. Both Lucy and I will be forever indebted to this godly woman for the personal help and training we received from her. Things she imparted to us both directly and indirectly by her life are lessons we have continued to draw on with profit and benefit to this day."

Lila Trotman lives in Colorado near the Nav headquarters. Her children are all married and living in various parts of the United States. She speaks with pride of her oldest son Bruce and his wife Jeanette, of her daughter Ruth and her husband George Wortley, of her son Burke and his wife Diana, and daughter Faith and husband David Kraft. She refers to her "in-laws" as her "in-loves"; and, acknowledges the need these children and precious nine grandchildren have filled in her life.

Of this remarkable woman one can say many things. God has

given to her some of life's choicest experiences, but also some of life's greatest heartaches. Through it all, the verse which has meant so much to her, shows the beauty of her soul and the integrity of her heart. One can only stand back in respectful awe, thanking God for the example of her life, and trusting him to allow the telling of her story to serve as a blessing and challenge to others to follow in the steps of such a woman of God.

Of her life since Dawson's homegoing, Lila speaks without bitterness, and it seems fitting that the final words of her story should come from herself: "I'm sure because Dawson founded The Navigators, and because the name Trotman is known in so many Christian circles, that often it is expected that I know the answers because Dawson did! Years ago it came to me that I wasn't left here to be a Dawson Trotman. He had the ability of meeting a plane or train, conducting a Bible study here, rushing off to one, two or three breakfasts, greeting guests and having flowers or fruit in their room, dictating letters, entertaining, making on-the-spot decisions, and I could go on and on—*but*, I am to be Lila, *in Christ and for Christ.* God's grace is sufficient, and *my* whole dependence must be on him and his enabling. All I truly want is that HE alone be honored. I know God uses us, his people—but also, I know without him, I'd be nothing."

Cameo thirteen

"Can God Be This Real?"

Darlene Swanson

When Darlene Janzen was three days old she was pronounced dead. The doctor took her out of the incubator and telephoned the tragic news to her father. As Mr. Janzen raced to the hospital he prayed: "O God, let it be a mistake. Let her live, and if you do we will never hold her back from whatever you, God, want her to do."

Mr. Janzen quickly looked up the doctor who said, "Oh, Mr. Janzen, I'm sorry we alarmed you. The nurse rechecked the baby, thought she detected a spark of life, and put her back into the incubator!"

Darlene doesn't know if the doctor made a mistake, but she does know that she is alive today—really alive. She believes that God let her live for a reason and a purpose. And lest others think she is somehow different, she points out that everyone alive today could have had his life snuffed out at some time or another. She believes that God has a definite purpose for every person. She says: "God created us and has given each of us unique abilities and talents and wants us to use them. He wants to bring out the best in us. It is not a sign of weakness to depend on Almighty God; it is a sign of wisdom."

But the role Darlene Swanson finds herself living today is far different from that which she had imagined for herself a few years ago. She studied piano for seventeen years in order to be a concert pianist. Dreams of fame and fortune were uppermost in her thinking and their achievement at her very fingertips when she made a life-changing discovery.

That discovery was to turn this beautiful young woman from the path of Hollywood fame to a global trail of service for God. Today, as the wife of David Swanson, vice-president of S. B. Thomas, Inc. (Speciality Bakers since 1880), Darlene finds life even more challenging and exciting than any dream she had in her pre-Hollywood days. Engagements have taken her into twenty-two countries as pianist and speaker; and with her husband she reaches out to U.S. teen-agers. Twice-a-month rallies are held to reach the teen-agers of Long Island— meetings that draw thousands. This is the way Darlene tells her fascinating story.

* * * * *

I began studying the piano at age five. I wanted to be a concert pianist more than anything else in the world, and spent long hours studying and practicing. When I was twelve I played the lead piano with a fifteen-piano ensemble in our hometown in California's San Joaquin Valley. The conductor of the NBC Symphony Orchestra in Hollywood came to conduct the group; it was exciting to be the youngest one and playing the lead piano. I thought: This is great, to be on the stage entertaining people! When I was sixteen I gave my debut concert.

I went to church every Sunday because Mom and Dad took us to church every Sunday! Unfortunately, we were in a church where we heard more of the traditions of the church than of the reality of Christ. I began to rebel, thinking, "I'll go my own way, I'll be a lot happier." I stopped attending church. I just hadn't seen the dynamic vitality that Jesus Christ can add to a person's life.

I had been studying with Ezma Miller, and then Noah Steinberg of Germany. In Los Angeles I studied with Dr. Roy Ried Brignall, F.T.C.L. from the Trinity College Royal Conservatory of England, who was a pupil of Tobias Matthay, as was Myra Hess. It was a great privilege to study under these great men, to do concerts and perform.

While in college I was asked to appear on the Hollywood TV Guest Hour program. A producer saw me and I was signed into

Screen Actor's Guild—of which I am still a member—and did my first film. I quickly learned how much money one could make in acting, and I began to pursue acting as a career, studying drama at night in Pasadena Playhouse.

When I got my own apartment in Hollywood, I thought, "Oh, how exciting, how glamorous! This is really living!" I had gone to school with "Fred Flintstone" and "Wilma," and in those days it was a status symbol to have one's own heated swimming pool, which I had. I thought, "I've *really* arrived!"

But there was one thing I had not counted on—I had to live with *me*. Frequently I returned to that apartment at night, looked up at the ceiling and said, "God, if you really do exist and you really made me, then what did you create me for? I entertain people for a few hours and then they go right back to their same problems and same troubles. There must be something more to life than just trying to make a name for myself. It seems unreal!"

There's a wonderful verse of Scripture which says, "Seek and ye shall find; knock and it shall be opened unto you" (Matthew 7:7). I was seeking, whether I realized it or not. When God created us he put a vacuum in our hearts which can only be filled by himself. We are restless, like a piano out of tune, until we let him come in. Many times we don't understand this restlessness; but there is an anxiety, a loneliness and only God can fill that. "Seek and ye shall find." I was seeking! I didn't realize it then, but a person never gets away from the teachings of godly parents. How I thank God for my parents!

It was at this time that I met Roy and Dale Rogers, who invited me to their home for a Bible study for actors and actresses. They dared to be different! I went, out of curiosity, because I frankly didn't believe people in show business would be that interested in studying the Bible. But I went for another reason. They asked me to play the piano—and one never knows who will be around to hear and see the performance!

The prayer time that evening was so new to me that I could hardly believe what I was hearing. These fifty or sixty actors and actresses took turns praying—many of them thanking God for answered prayer. Some had experienced answers that same day! And I thought, "Can God be *this real*, that a person can experience an answer to prayer every day?"

Then they thanked God for being able to share their faith with cameramen and people on the set. And I thought, "Can God be *this real*, that you'd want to stick your neck out and share your faith with a makeup man? Why, he's likely to blackball you in putting on your makeup! Can God be *this real*, that you'd want to share him with everyone? What's the difference between these people and me? I think I'm a Christian. I believe in God. I believe in Christ. I've been to church most of my life—what's the difference? These people have something real and I don't have it, and I want it."

Sometime later I heard a speaker discuss a Scripture verse that showed me the difference between believing that God and Christ exist and *really* believing in them. The verse is John 1:12, "But as many as received him, to them gave he power to become the sons of God, even to them that believe on his name."

He explained that God gave us the freedom to choose or reject him; he'll never force us to love him. He loves us so dearly! "And to as many as receive him"—a definite act of faith, not an emotion but a commitment of ourselves to him—"to them he gives the power to become children of God, even to them who believe on his name."

God will not cramp our style—I love to tell that to teen-agers—he'll enhance it! He'll give us the dimension to living that he wanted us to have when he made us. He takes our talents and our abilities, sometimes ones we never knew we possessed and brings them out, because we have God-confidence, not self-confidence. The ego goes, and it's in God that we have faith and trust, and we have peace that's beyond understanding.

I stayed in Hollywood a few years after that. Then one evening I was asked to go to New Zealand with a forerunner team of the Billy Graham Crusade. I thought, "Leave Hollywood and my career?" My agent said, "This is ridiculous; you've just been offered a contract to do a series of television films in which you'll be acting. This will be the making of your career. The evangelist will be reaching these people anyway; look at the people you can reach if you stay here and work with the Hollywood Christian group!"

It's easy to rationalize, but I knew I'd never be happy unless I was in the center of God's will and doing what he wanted me to do. After much prayer, I went to New Zealand. I was trembling as I boarded that plane, but I thank God I went! Corrie Ten Boom, a women who helped liberate thousands of Jewish people through the Dutch underground in World War II, was on the team and I learned much from her. It was my growing process; God showed me so many things on that trip.

The pace was exacting, with some days having as many as seven different meetings, including a radio contract for three programs a week on New Zealand B.B.C. So, enroute home, I stopped for a few days of rest in Hawaii. The last morning of the stopover I was up early and decided to read the newspaper on the beach. The beauty of God's creation and the quiet of the morning filled my heart with praise for God. Unable to concentrate on the news, I put the paper down and noticed that I was no longer alone. Nearby was a little man on a beach mat. He was short and rather stocky and was wearing big, horn-rimmed glasses. I looked at him and in my friendliest tone of voice called out, "Aloha! Would you like to read the morning paper? I'm going for a swim."

He answered—in what I was certain was his grouchiest voice—"I've read it already!"

I thought to myself, "Boy, I know why he's out here at this hour—his wife can't stand him!"

Then he startled me by adding, "I'm sorry; forgive me for sounding like that. You see, I'm the editor of the morning paper and I just got off work." His manner changed as he smiled and said, "What are you doing here?"

I explained to him why I was in Hawaii. "You—a missionary?" His disbelief was evident.

He wanted a story, but I had to refuse. "I'm scheduled for a guest appearance on TV this afternoon, and then I'm leaving. But if I am ever back in Hawaii I'll knock on your door and we can do that story."

I didn't know that I would be back in two weeks as music director for radio station KAIM, and with my own radio program: "Darlene At The Baldwin," and also to do a TV series.

Keeping my promise to Eddy Sherman, the newspaper editor, on my return, I went to his office. Anticipating an unusual story, he warmly welcomed me. During the interview he said, "You really believe this—that Christ was the Messiah—don't you? How do you know?"

I answered, "I know because Christianity works! No other man has made history date itself back to the time after his birth. . . ."

He replied, "You know, that's good enough for me! Will you help me pray?" And with that he invited Jesus Christ into his life and accepted him as the Messiah promised to Israel. Later I assisted Eddy Sherman on his "Backstage" program, interviewing celebrities who come to the Island. Afterward we would take them out for dinner (our sponsor owned a restaurant). This offered opportunities to talk to such celebrities as Lucille Ball, Desi Arnez, Robert Mitchum, June Allyson and Dick Powell, explaining what I believed.

I was asked to be in the musical *South Pacific* being filmed on the Islands; but I had already made plans to go to Copenhagen to play the piano for the Youth for Christ World Congress. I'm so glad I went because Billy Graham asked me to stop on the way and help with the Crusade in Madison Square Garden—and it was there I met my future husband!

Dave Swanson, as a businessman, was helping in the Crusade in May, 1957, and at that time he committed his life to Christ. In July I came along and we met. Dave had never heard of Youth for Christ, but he called the president and made arrangements for a visa so that later, when I boarded the chartered plane for the Copenhagen YFC Youth Congress, there he was! We had 104 delegates chaperoning—as it were—but that was the beginning, and later on I became Mrs. David Swanson!

After we had been married for two years our first son was born prematurely and not expected to live. At first I spent much time fretting and fussing. Then I became quite tired because the baby had to be fed every three hours—and it took him two hours to drink four ounces of milk! Many times I looked at my husband and thought, "Oh, can't you get up and help once in awhile!" And then I'd say to the Lord, "I don't even have time to get alone with you anymore. It's just ridiculous!" And the glow of life began to go. Then the Lord quietly indicated that I should "make my interruptions my opportunities!" He showed me that no time could be more quiet than two a.m. and five a.m. in the morning when I was feeding that dear little life he had given me. And those hours that had been tiresome became precious, looked-for moments. Yes, God is real and relevant to everyday living; he wants to be a part of every life.

It's thrilling to see teen-agers and women come to know Jesus Christ and then let God direct their lives! I know nothing that is more exciting! It's thrilling to see what is happening all over the world! I believe every Christian should ask God to give him a job so big that unless he undertakes it you are sunk!

I'm so thankful to have a husband who feels he should practice Christian principles in his business. It's not easy in our competitive world. My husband felt, as did his brothers, that it was important to have a Bible study in the bakery. Once a week they meet for prayer and Bible study with the staff, and, once a month the secretaries have a catered luncheon and speakers come in. It has been amazing to see the response and interest. When they opened a new wholesale company in New Jersey the first thing asked was, "When do we start such groups here?".

I'm thankful, too, that my husband encourages me to go out and speak for the Lord. We also do a lot of this together. A home built around the Word is so wonderful! We all have problems whether we are Christians or not; but it is great, as husband and wife, to face our problems—and then together take them to the Lord!

We are actively supporting the youth work of Jim Vaus, and serve on the board of his Youth Development, Inc., a social welfare agency in Harlem, New York. When the project began, a businessman donated money for a beauty shop and a girl friend and I went to work with the girls from teen-age gangs. We fixed their hair, taught them how to apply makeup, and how to use silverware. We discovered some of them had never eaten with a fork, knife or spoon! With consistent love we were able to win their confidence and tell them about our Lord.

Many of them accepted him. Now, some nine years later, it is interesting to note that although the crime rate has gone up in New York City, the crime rate has dropped about ten percent in that one square mile where 145,000 people live.

It is a privilege to be a Representative at Large for Christian Women's Clubs International. I had the joy of being the first Chairman on Long Island. When I was asked to participate in the work of this organization, I had just been married and I said, "Oh, no, I want to work with teen-agers; I don't have time to get involved with women's clubs." But then I went to some area meetings and was tremendously impressed. What a great method for reaching women! The women involved are given an opportunity to use their talents for God and also to help other women to speak with confidence to their neighbors and friends.

And so I accepted the chairmanship on Long Island and later in New Jersey. Eventually our Long Island Club grew to 600 and divided into three groups. Why has God so blessed the work of CWC? Not because of any one person, but because groups of women, all interested in the same God, are willing to work very hard together to let the Lord be known in the community.

We are interested in the work of International Christian Leadership. And it's been my privilege to play for the Annual Congressional Wives' Prayer Breakfast (while the Annual Presidential Prayer Breakfast is held) for the past nine years. I have set to music II Chronicles 7:14 as a prayer for our country. It is entitled *If My People* and is used as the benediction each year for the Prayer Breakfast. How much we need to know the reality of the words: "If my people, which are called by my name, shall humble themselves, and pray, and seek my face, and turn from their wicked ways; then will I hear from heaven, and will forgive their sin, and will heal their land."

When Jerome Hines sang at President Kennedy's last Prayer Breakfast, I accompanied him on the piano. There has also been opportunity to speak to many prayer groups of Congressional wives, State Department secretaries, and some in the Pentagon. After the 1968 Congressional Wives' Prayer Breakfast I was asked to attend the Military Wives' Luncheon. At the head table were the wives of the Chiefs of Staff and Chaplains' wives. I was quite nervous and let this be known to God. It was as though he said to me, "Well, Darlene, I have you here not because you're a great speaker, but to share the peace of God available to an anxious world."

My favorite verses of Scripture are Philippians 4:4-7. "Rejoice in the Lord always; again will I say, rejoice. Let all men know of your forbearance (we are to be witnesses). The Lord is at hand (he's real). (Therefore) have no anxiety about anything, but in everything by prayer and supplication with thanksgiving let your requests be made known to God. And the peace of God, which passes all understanding, will keep your hearts and minds through Christ Jesus."

This is the peace you and I daily need in our lives, and it comes only through Jesus Christ. Yes, God loves us so dearly "that he gave his only begotten Son, that whosoever believeth in him should not perish, but have everlasting life." Oh, how he loves us!

I've had teen-agers say to me, "Well, if he loves us so much, why did he make a hell?"

I reply, "Let's think positively. He loves us so much he's doing everything in the world to keep us from going there. He loved us so much he gave his most prized possession, Jesus Christ, to be the Savior to pay for our sins, that we might know him. But not only did he do that, he sent his Son into this world to live and to be human that he might understand, know what we think, and how we feel. He allowed Jesus to be a baby, a child, a teen-ager. He allowed him to be a professional man—a carpenter, a breadwinner—so he knows all about balancing the budget. He knows the strains that are placed on a mother.

"When we invite him into our lives, that instant we are his child and can know it. He knows what we are thinking and feeling. Have you ever wished someone could understand and identify with you? He can! The Bible says, 'For we have not an high priest who is unable to sympathize with our weaknesses, but one who in every respect has been tempted as we are, yet without sinning. Let us then with confidence (boldly) draw near to the throne of grace, that we may receive mercy and find grace to help in time of need' (Hebrews 4:15-16).

"This is what the world needs! He's interested in the most important things that happen to us, as well as the little things.

And when you are a child of the King of all kings, you're never insignificant, you're special! Don't limit God in your life!"

Sometime ago, the night before I was to leave on a speaking engagement, I was tucking our two little boys in bed and Davey said, "Mommy, I just can't sleep." And I said, "Honey, what's wrong? Can't we talk about it?" And so we did.

Davey said, "Mommy, can't God send some other mommy to tell those ladies about Jesus just this once?"

I said to him, "Dear, if there were more mommies who would tell other mommies about Jesus, then I wouldn't have to go. You're glad that Mommy could tell you about Jesus, and that he lives in your heart."

Davey answered, "Yes, Mommy, I'm glad. But can't he send some other mommy, just this one time?" Now he was sobbing. By this time I was crushed. I silently prayed: "Lord, I can't leave unless you give me the answer." At such times God is so real and precious, and makes me know he loves me and is interested in every detail of my life. He gave me this to tell Davey, "You know, Davey, God loved us so much he let his little boy come down to earth, leaving all the go-carts (which Davey happens to love) and other good things behind. He lived here thirty-three years so that he might understand us, and then he died to pay for our mistakes. Don't you think if God could let his little boy do that, you could let Mommy go for three days?"

Davey looked at me and said, "OK, Mom, you go and I'll pray."

* * * * *

With children, teen-agers or women, Darlene's chief concern is that Jesus be real to them—that he guide their lives. She emphasizes that by faith in Christ a person can belong to God and then receive the love and peace that every heart longs for.

Not all of us, like Darlene, can talk personally to the First Lady of the land, nor jet to distant parts of the world and participate in crusades and youth congresses. To very few is given the privilege of serving as co-chairman for the special performance of Jerome Hines' opera, *I Am The Way,* at the Metropolitan Opera in Lincoln Center, New York City. Only a few can assist Jerome Hines and movie producer Erwin S. Yeoworth, Jr., in forming a nationwide organization to be known as The Fellowship of Christians in the Arts, Media, and

Entertainment. The majority of people will never have such experiences, but everyone reading Darlene's story can know that God is real and relevant to every need, because Darlene has proved it. Circumstances in life differ, but each person can be the child of the King of all kings, as Darlene Swanson has discovered. Each person is special to God, regardless of residence, occupation, or age. Yes, God is *this real!*

Cameo fourteen

A Wing And
Her Prayer

Betty Truxton

For the nomadic life in store for her, Elizabeth (Betty) Clarke came from a very settled home background. It was a devout home where . regular church attendance was as expected as mealtime. As she grew up in Washington, D.C., Betty was spiritually helped by an able Sunday school teacher, Ruth Fisher, and also by some Baptist Student Union Bible studies that were led by several people. Upon graduation from high school she attended the University of Maryland for five years where she received her nurse's training and a B.S. degree. A personally rewarding time followed her college graduation as she served with the Visiting Nurses Association in the poorer, low-income districts.

In 1943 Betty joined the United States Army as an Army nurse, and was soon sent to England. While she was beginning her career as an Army nurse, a certain Navy man was sharing with his buddies his dream of helping missionaries with his aviation experience. Betty had no way of knowing then that this man and his dream would one day come into her life.

Jim Truxton, while stationed at Floyd Bennett Field, New York, talked with two other Navy pilots who shared his vision of using airplanes where surface transportation was poor or topographical barriers were a major obstacle to mission advance. Encouraged by a missionary friend to whom they disclosed their ideas, Jim was chosen, even while the war was in progress, to set in motion an organization for missionary flying purposes. Thus began Missionary Aviation Fellowship—and this beginning accounts for MAF's readiness to go into action promptly after the war ended.

And even as God was preparing Jim for postwar activities, he was preparing Betty. Her unit was sent to France. Here she began attending Bible studies for military personnel held in the French home of Mr. and Mrs. Pons. During these studies, the Word of God spoke forcefully to her heart. The studies whet her spiritual appetite. One evening she told the group of her newly aroused desire to commit her life to the Lord—of her increasing hunger to know the Lord more wholly and personally and to find a more definite sense of direction in her life.

Because of the influence of these wartime Bible studies, when Betty returned to the States after the war, she decided to seek further training—with missionary service as her goal. Her choice of Eastern Baptist Seminary, where Jim's married brother Addison was a student, was surely providential. God was directing.

During these years Jim Truxton, busy for the Navy in Okinawa, still had managed to pioneer the work of the fledgling organization then known as CAMF (Christian Airman's Missionary Fellowship). Through a magazine article by Betty Greene (a Women's Air Force Service Pilot—WASP) in the Inter-Varsity Christian Fellowship publication *His,* Jim Truxton had learned of her desire to use her flying in missions. Through subsequent contact Betty Greene agreed to open the Los Angeles CAMF office, convinced of God's call .

When the war ended, Jim was in Japan with the occupation forces. In November of 1945, his tour of duty was up, and with expectant excitement he, at last, stepped into he CAMF office.

In the spring of 1946 Jim found himself desperately needing assistance. He increasingly felt the Lord's prompting to enlist the help of a fellow airman, Charlie Mellis, an Army pilot with many B-17 missions over Germany. Charlie, with his wife Claire, had returned to complete his remaining two years at Wheaton College. To Jim's great joy Charlie Mellis agreed to move and head up the Los Angeles office.

This move freed Jim to travel the country seeking support, enlisting recruits, and discussing with mission leaders the objectives of the organization whose name was legally changed to Missionary Aviation Fellowship. MAF's basic premise of using highly trained aviation specialists to cooperatively serve missions evolved out of these talks. Almost simultaneously the companion MAF groups of England and Australia had formed, and then New Zealand's supporting MAF Council.

Meanwhile, Jim's younger brother Addison wrote from Eastern Baptist Seminary enthusiastically telling Jim of a young lady he believed to be Jim's "dream girl." Addison had observed in the lovely Betty Clarke, qualities that he knew his brother would want in a wife. In her, he sensed an inner as well as outward beauty, and that she shared with Jim a determination to find and to follow the will of God. He urged Jim to include Eastern on his East Coast itinerary—and for more than deputational purposes!

Upon Jim's arrival, with only one free evening in the area, Addison lost no time in introducing them. But when Jim invited Betty to spend the evening with him, she hesitated. A fellow student, Ruth Swain, had two tickets for the concert, and had already asked Betty to go with her. However, when Ruth learned that Jim had asked Betty out for the evening, she insisted Betty and Jim use her tickets. That made two cupids at work!

As Betty recounts it: "The evening was marvelous! Jim was everything a girl could desire on an initial date. Following the concert, we spent the rest of the evening talking about his work and things of the Lord. I found myself strongly attracted to Jim, and remember questioning my right to be so drawn to him on a first meeting. My enthusiasm for his work was great, but there was something about him—a difference—a deep sense of purpose, a relating of all of life to the plan and will of God that greatly appealed to me."

There was no doubt about the mutual response one for the other. Jim sensed that his brother's assessment had been a true one. Before leaving that evening he asked and secured Betty's promise to correspond.

Even before his itineration for MAF was finished, Betty

began receiving letters from Jim—long, newsy letters—letters
full of his joy in being in the Lord's service. But they were
letters, too, which indicated his personal interest in Betty:
"Well, Betty, it's about time to bring this lengthy epistle to a
close. Sure has been nice to talk with you by letter, though I
can't help wishing it could be in person. . . . It would be mighty
nice to hear from you, Betty, any time you can find a few free
minutes. . . ."

Betty *was* finding those "few free minutes!" In fact, they
were becoming more than a few! And thus began their
courtship by correspondence. The "dates on paper" which Jim
had asked for every now and then became increasingly frequent,
until they were able to meet again the following summer—after
which time the correspondence was to resume once again.

Jim was busy. Still, he found time to share by letter his
heartfelt hopes for the great work and open doors which lay
before them as an organization dedicated to serve missions. As
he related the many meaningful experiences he was having he
couldn't help saying, "Sure wish you could be having these
experiences with me." Deep within her heart Betty was
beginning to share the same wishful thinking!

Betty shared Jim's enthusiasm about the MAF work and
inquired about the possibility of using her nursing experience
on the field. He was quick to impress upon her the need for
missionary nurses. Of her letters he said: "Your letters are like a
nice cool drink of water after a day's trek over a parched desert
. . . I tell you, Betty, it's great to run across someone who thinks
.as seriously and earnestly as you do about the proper type of
preparation for a specific missionary job."

Then came an invitation from Jim inviting Betty to visit him
and his family in Los Angeles after school was out. Her reply
indicated a desire to do so if arrangements could be made. His
answer gave strong indication of his feelings: "When the idea
first occurred to me I hardly dared think of it as being a
possibility. I just knew that I wanted very much to renew our
companionship too abruptly terminated in Philadelphia. I do
hope and pray that you can come, and am confident that if this
is in the will of the Lord he will make a way, so long as we are
alert to the means he provides." Jim was endeavoring to be alert

to God's leading both for Betty and himself, as well as for the work to which he felt so called.

Wanting only to be in the Lord's will, Betty prayed and looked for some tangible means that would indicate that she should make the trip to see Jim. Then a group of students traveling west offered Betty a ride—and she felt free to make definite plans to go with them. Jim wrote from Mexico, "I'm glad you feel perfectly at peace about coming to California, and confident of the Lord's pleasure in it. I wouldn't want you to come otherwise. . . . Again, I'm very frank to say that I am looking forward with great joy to seeing you again, especially in view of the fact that I may have quite a long tour ahead of me in South America. I'd really like to become better acquainted with the one whose letters have meant so much to me, and have been a source of encouragement and delight.

"I do hope your family will be wholeheartedly in accord with your making the trip. I'm not a bit surprised at their first reaction, and can hardly blame them for wondering who this "yardbird" Truxton is anyway, and why, after a single date you'd give the guy a second thought, much less make a trip across the country to see him. All I can suggest to you, and to them, is that things do not always run according to the usual cut and dry pattern in this life of ours. In fact, the things that find their way into print, in story, into folklore, etc., even history itself, are often the unusual, even unconventional things. Then, when God comes into the picture, there is added reason for the unexpected and unusual. . . ."

Jim had arranged for Betty to stay with a nurse friend—who later married Nate Saint. Marjorie Farris was her name then (now Van Der Puy, see the Marj Saint Van Der Puy story elsewhere in this book), and she invited Betty to share an adjoining room in the nurse quarters at Luthern Hospital in downtown Los Angeles.

The three-week stay in L.A. confirmed what their hearts had been saying from the moment they met. Jim's family loved Betty from the outset, as did the MAF staff. Each evening, when Betty returned to the room in the nurses quarters, Marj Farris would ask, "Has he proposed yet?" Betty smiled shyly and answered, "When he does, I'll put a rose on your pillow."

On Sunday afternoon, only a few days remained before Betty was due to leave for the East Coast, Jim had taken her to the Long Beach Municipal Auditorium to hear the Old Fashioned Revival Hour broadcast. The last song was: "No One Ever Cared For Me Like Jesus." As they left, Jim steered Betty toward the horseshoe pier beside the auditorium. Hand in hand, they walked out some distance, their hearts still stirred by both the message and the music. The thought of soon separating, however, brought a painful stab to each of their hearts ... and they were silent for some while. And then it came: the proposal to which Betty's heart had so yearned to respond! The following morning Marjorie Farris found the rose Betty had promised on her pillow!

Then they had to separate. Jim's duties called him to South America and Betty returned to Eastern to complete her studies. The stream of correspondence began again—but now with many a tender exchange and sentiment.

As a surprise Jim had arranged for Betty's mother to place a lovely, leather Mexican jewelry box with the engagement ring inside among her gifts on Christmas Day, 1947. They were also to tune in on short wave to Radio Station HCJB to hear Christmas greetings from Jim. He had once told Betty that when it came time to announce their engagement he would shout it from the rooftops. He literally did that very thing— joyously telling 'the world' on the *Back Home Hour Program* from Quito, Ecuador, that he and Elizabeth Clarke were engaged!

In one of her letters Betty asked Jim to outline some of the ways in which she would be able to help him after they were married. This he did, then jokingly added, "Now I'm making it look as if all I'm marrying you for is to have a secretary to do my typing and a nurse to keep me well—strictly business. Well, you just marry me and see how 'strictly business' it is! Seriously, dear, there are so many other ways in which I need you. There will be times when just the encouragement and cheer of your smile will be used of God to mean success when there might have been failure; to make many a dark day or discouraging experience a bit easier to bear.... Then, your sensitive, thoughtful heart may help me to avoid a careless mistake, remind me of some of the little things (which are so often big) that men are prone to forget. In this work I'm going to have to deal with couples, not just men, and here I know I'll need your advice many times. Problems which I've not yet had to face will be easier because we experience them together and can talk them over frankly. Oh, sweetheart, a man just isn't complete without a wife. That's why God made a woman so dear and precious as you, because he saw how many things this guy lacked. . . !"

As the time came for Betty to write her thesis, she thought: why not write on "Aviation in Missions." Jim agreed, "This way we can 'kill two birds with one stone' . . . I've wanted to tell you all about the organization into which, in a very real sense, you will be marrying. The background will help you appreciate the present. I shall be delighted to help all I can."

Betty completed her studies—and her thesis, which was marvelous orientation for a future MAF wife! God, in his goodness, made it possible for Jim to join Betty's parents for her graduation from Eastern Baptist Seminary.

A few weeks later, on June 19, 1948, they were married. Their wedding was everything they had prayed it might be. Particularly outstanding, to them, was the brief missionary message by the pastor just before the ceremony began.

Among the family members present was Jim's Aunt Virginia Campbell, who had served the Lord in Egypt. More than any other one person, she had influenced Jim to accept Christ as his Savior while in his teens. Another aunt, Margaret Truxton, from Philadelphia, described the wedding this way: "I never heard vows more beautifully spoken, especially by Betty. She was perfectly calm and composed, and spoke so clearly and emphatically . . . brides rarely speak out so they are heard. It was a double ring ceremony. Dr. Harris gave a lovely prayer . . . beautiful thoughts reverently and sincerely spoken, a sort of consecration prayer covering their future work. Pastor Hurlburt then pronounced the benediction, something I had never heard at a wedding. Betty was radiant in her white organza gown . . . there was no glamour . . . and it seemed as if we were on hallowed ground; we felt as if we'd been let in on something sacred."

For their honeymoon Jim and Betty had been offered an age-old country estate near Philadelphia. While Jim was looking over the house before the wedding, a long black snake wriggled its way across the doorpost! But, it proved an ideal setting—and even good missionary orientation! They really roughed it: chopped wood for outdoor cooking, picked wild strawberries, heard all kinds of spooky, creaking noises in the old mansion at night—but they never did see the snake. Marj and Nate Saint (now married) joined the honeymooners for one afternoon of fun and talk.

The time soon came for Nate Saint and Jim to fly the first MAF Stinson plane to Ecuador to be put into missionary service. Betty, who flew down by commercial airliner with Marj, was rapidly initiated into life on a developing mission base. Upon visiting Shell Mera, where the fellows and Charlie Mellis' dad (now approaching his 70th birthday) were building the Saint's home, she and Jim shared a canvas tent as another honeymoon hideaway.

Charged with the task of initial survey to determine the feasibility and then the shape of needed MAF service in a given country or area, Jim and Betty were constantly on the move: Ecuador to Colombia, to Venezuela—then Venezuela to the U.S., back south again to Brazil, Guyana, and back to Brazil. Three suitcases and a footlocker were soon battered, and several times replaced. Whether "home" was just a curtained-off area in the kitchen of a missionary friend, two cots in an otherwise unfurnished room, or an oil company field-office trailer, Betty and Jim continually made new discoveries as to their human frailty, and of the divine resources upon which they could draw.

They saw in others, as well as in themselves, the weaknesses that a faithful Creator was continually transforming. They saw the beauty of human clay revealed in the missionaries' heartcry for the lost. They saw the Potter choose "foolish things of the world to confound the wise . . . the weak things of the world to confound the things which are mighty . . . and base things of the world—things despised—to bring to nought things that are" (I Corinthians 1:27-28).

Betty can look back on many rich and meaningful experiences that she shared with Jim in the Lord's service. But, two times of crisis are particularly imprinted on her mind because the reality of God's presence and grace were most abundantly proven.

The first occurred soon after the Shell Mera home was completed. Nate and Marj went up to Quito for the Christmas holidays and to await the arrival of their first child. Betty and Jim went to Shell Mera to "hold the fort" at the base. Writing home, they described the beautiful tree they trimmed with the colorful Christmas cards of loved ones and friends: "The effect was lovely, and we appreciated it so much because it was adorned with so many warm and loving expressions . . . it made us feel very close to you at home. . . ."

But the calm of this glorious season was shaken a few days later by the violent crash of the Stinson. Nate was the pilot and Mrs. Wilfred Tidmarsh, an expectant missionary mother, and her young son were on board. They had just taken off into the tricky air of Quito's 9,300 foot airport elevation.

News of the accident was instantly relayed through the Shell Oil Company, and Betty and Jim rushed to Quito. Apart from Nate's injured back (requiring almost six months in a cumbersome plaster cast) injuries were miraculously light. A few days later Marj Saint gave birth to their first child, Kathy. And a few months later Mrs. Tidmarsh gave birth to an unharmed and perfect child. Betty was grateful for her nursing experience which made it possible for her to help both of these women.

With their airplane demolished, the two fellows were hit hard by this sudden and seemingly early end to all they had labored so hard to build. It was then that both Betty and Marj became vessels in God's hands to buoy their husband's spirits, and to help keep the "lamp" of faith shining bright.

Within three months air service was restored to the jungle missionary outposts. But in numerous other ways God demonstrated the meaning of his promise: "We know that all that happens to us is working for our good if we love God, and if we are fitting into his plans" (Romans 8:28, *Living New Testament, Paraphrased*). Out of this crucible grew MAF's now highly specialized flight orientation of all their overseas missionary airmen.

The second crisis came almost seven years later in early December, 1955. Betty and Jim were returning to the U.S. from Brazil. They made a special point of flying via Ecuador to visit Nate and Marj at Shell Mera. Jim soon sensed that momentous happenings were in the wind. Nate enthusiastically revealed that the plan for establishing peaceful contact with the hostile, but long-prayed-for, Auca tribe was well underway. Carefully Nate went over each detail: the exchanging of gifts by "bucket-drop" corkscrewing down on the end of a 1,600 foot nylon line from the plane circling about 500 feet above, the signs of Auca expectancy and diminishing hostility, the possible landing site near the village, etc. . . .

That night Betty noticed that Jim, weary as he was, lay awake for a long time—and it was the same the next night. Though not yet aware of the details of the Auca contact plan, she instinctively knew he was carrying a heavy burden of responsibility—a preoccupation of some kind. As an officer of MAF he could have advised or required that the plan be dropped—or at least delayed for further examination. She quietly prayed that God would give him needed wisdom, and perfect peace whatever might transpire.

Finally it was time for them to continue on to Fullerton, California, where Jim was eager to confer with his top MAF colleagues. Together there was a confidence and mutual sharing of what Jim has stated many times since: "If any other group of missionaries had shared in the decades of prayer for the Aucas, had wrestled with and discarded many plans for reaching them, had known the non-mission exploitation of Aucas that would result in dead or even more hostile Aucas—had they experienced, as the five fellows did, the accumulative evidences of God's hand preparing the way—they could hardly have turned their backs upon this clear summons of God!"

Why, then, were Betty and Jim almost overwhelmed by the martyrdom? They had been so confident of a successful outcome. Why? They had viewed the situation with human eyes—eyes of faith—but still human. And, having been with the Saints less than a month before, they could not shake a terrifying sense of responsibility. Jim confided to Betty: "My whole insides feel like they have turned into one solid, heavy rock pulling me down." She then remembered the prayer that night in the Saint's home—and again she prayed for perfect peace.

That peace did come in due time, but first to Betty. Increasingly her peace was imparted to Jim—and their experience in this recalls what he had written during their courtship correspondence: "... there are so many ways in which I need you. There will be times when just the encouragement and cheer of your smile will be used of God to mean success when there might have been failure; to make many a dark day or discouraging experience a bit easier to bear. . . ."

Succeeding years, familiar to all who have followed the accounts, have demonstrated how gloriously successful "operation Auca" really was—encompassing and affecting so much more than just "Auca territory!"

Today, as younger couples are the ones to open up, survey, and blaze the new trails, Betty enjoys the opportunity of extending hospitality after years of Jim and her being the happy recipients. Their Fullerton hillside home is frequently the haven of travel-weary missionaries and other friends, the scene of missionary orientation discussions, a relaxed game and get-acquainted night with missionary candidates, a joyous hymn-sing, or even the gleeful shouts of MAF children to many of whom she and Jim have become "Aunt" and "Uncle." Now, instead of playing the accordion, Betty plays the piano—and enjoys giving lessons to MAF and other children.

Betty knows and is concerned that others know that she is one of many women who in their quiet, unassuming and devoted way have been a tower of strength to their husbands. These women have discovered, as Betty did, the truth of God's promise: "Trust in the Lord with all thine heart; and lean not unto thine own understanding. In all thy ways acknowledge him, and he shall direct thy paths" (Proverbs 3:5-6).

Cameo fifteen

A Great Adventure

Vonette Bright

Vonette Bright, a 5'2", smiling brunette, has thought of herself as a modern-day Cinderella, though with some notable differences from the storybook princess. Whereas the fairy tale Cinderella, for example, had a very unhappy childhood, Vonette Zachary grew up in the security and loving warmth of a happy home. As the oldest of four children living in an Oklahoma town, her earliest recollections include all the activities of a wholesome life.

And, unlike Cinderella, Vonette didn't recognize romance when it first appeared. Sitting in the back of the school auditorium as an eighth-grader, Vonette watched and listened to an outstanding student, several grades ahead of her, as he gave a narration prepared for a contest. He had won a number of national speech honors, and as he spoke she thought, "He is so brilliant he could some day be president of the United States." Vonette wasn't romantically interested in the speaker, but found herself thinking, "I hope the man I marry will be as outstanding as it appears this fellow is likely to become." The Cinderella who sat among the cinders must have had similar idealistic notions about Prince Charming!

Years passed and this talented young man whose intelligence matched his name, Bill Bright, went on to college. Bill was gone, but an impression had been left upon the impressionable mind of a maturing girl. Whenever Bill returned home he was always free with his compliments toward Vonette, but she didn't take him seriously. "After all," she thought, "he's almost five years older than I."

Upon graduation from high school Vonette attended Texas State College for Women, majoring in home economics. Her church background and home training had prepared her morally. Early in her girlhood years she determined to save herself for the man she would someday marry, and that she would have no association before marriage which she would regret later. She set her standards high, and college did not change them.

Something else did change, however, as her thinking regarding Christianity wavered. She began to question the reality of Christianity. Her prayers seemed to get no further than the ceiling! In high school her major interest had been centered on church-related activities, but now Bible reading was meaningless—just so many words on a page. Doubts came creeping in. Her church attendance fell off. Restlessness drew her to bridge games, the movies or to Dallas to shop—anything to keep from being alone with her questions.

Then one sunny day, the summer after her freshman year in college, Vonette received a very special letter. The stationery was most impressive: "Bright's California Confections." Bill Bright was in business in California! A visit to the Coconut Grove, where he had seen a film star who reminded him of Vonette, had prompted the missive, he said. He hoped she'd have a nice summer—he would be thinking of her, he added. Thrilled over the letter, Vonette could hardly wait to share it with her father.

With a gleam in his eye, her dad replied, "Well, our hometown boy has gone away and made good. Now he's going to come home for his bride." Piqued, Vonette decided that in no way would she allow William Bright to think she was thrilled to hear from him! She decided to ignore the letter.

Somehow the letter managed to find its way into the things that went back to college with Vonette in the fall! One evening while cleaning out a desk drawer, she came across the letter. She began to share with her roommate some of her thoughts about this unusual young man from her hometown. The roommate's reply was, "You'd better write him—he sounds too good to pass up." It had been almost three years since she had seen the personable Bill Bright, but the rest of that evening was spent writing a ten-page letter to him!

That was the beginning, and what a romance it turned out to be! Air mail, special delivery letters started arriving. Correspondence flourished and before long the two were writing daily—Vonette highly recommends a romance by correspondence!

A very successful businessman now, Bill could be more generous than most of the suitors of college girls. Every week Vonette received flowers, candy, a telegram or telephone call, or something really outstanding. Her "beau" became the talk of campus. She says, "I was truly swept off my feet. What girl wouldn't have been? I knew by the time Bill arrived (he was coming in March), if he were the young man I remembered him to be, and the one he seemed to be from his conversations and his letters, I was in love."

When Bill arrived they had a delightful time together. After chatting about what had happened in the intervening years, he proposed marriage! They argue jokingly today about whether she said "yes" that first night or later, but, regardless, Cinderella was on her way.

It was almost three years before they were married. During this waiting period the spiritual questions began to plague her again. "Though I knew I was in love with Bill, there were many, many questions. I began to see that he was becoming firmly entrenched in his religious faith. He was sending me passages of Scripture to read, and they did not mean the same thing to me as they did to him. He would ask me to pray about certain things, and I knew it took someone far more devout than I to pray. I began to realize I was engaged to a man to whom Christianity meant a great deal, and yet it was not real to me. I was not being fair to myself or to him to think of devoting my life to teaching others something I did not believe myself. I decided Bill had become a religious fanatic, and that somehow he must be rescued from this fanaticism. I proceeded to attempt the rescue."

At the same time Bill was beginning to realize that perhaps Vonette was not a Christian. He knew he could not marry her until there was a change in her convictions. Knowing they were poles apart in this respect, yet loving her deeply, Bill encouraged her to come to California for a college briefing conference. It was 1948. Vonette's parents were opposed to her going though the engagement had been announced and the marriage was planned for September. Suddenly it appeared that the royal coach would turn back into a pumpkin; Cinderella hovered unsteadily on the brink of a fateful decision!

"Graduation day came," Vonette relates, "and as I walked across the stage to receive my degree a telegram from Bill was handed to me, simply congratulating me upon graduation from college. As I returned to my seat, I knew that I had to go to California."

Vonette's parents' hearts were softened, and so she boarded a train for California to visit her brother and Bill. "My parting words to my very best friend were that either Bill Bright would give up this fanaticism or I would come back without a ring. Little did I know what my trip held in store for me."

Immediately after arriving in Los Angeles, Bill and Vonette went to the college briefing conference at Forest Home, a Christian conference center in California. Here she met young people who possessed a quality of life she had never seen. They were vibrant and expressive regarding their faith. Feeling as she did that Christianity was something personal which one did not discuss freely, she was "bugged" by their statements. She tried to put their comments out of her mind, yet she admired them very much and liked the quality of life they evidenced.

"As I heard them make statements like, 'Let me tell you about my answer to prayer,' or 'Just look what I read in the Bible today!' I would ask them how they knew God had answered their prayers, or how they knew what the Bible really says. I especially wanted to find out how they knew God so personally.

"They would explain that their assurance was based on a personal relationship with Jesus Christ, God's Son. One evening as Bill and I were discussing what had taken place and the difference in these young people, I realized that his faith was right for him; but I had tried religion and it just wouldn't work for me. In no way did I want to stand in the way of his relationship to God, and I had come to the conclusion that perhaps the best thing to do was simply bow out of his life. I decided that at the end of the week I would return his ring, and we would go our separate ways."

But Vonette Zachary was destined to be Bill's wife, to share her life with a man who would found a ministry for God that would be felt around the world. God used Miss Henrietta Mears to reach this woman for himself—and for Bill.

Miss Mears was the inspiration and genius of the great Sunday school of the First Presbyterian Church of Hollywood, with its 6,000 members at that time. She was the founder of the Gospel Light Sunday school lessons, and because of her vision and efforts the conference grounds where Vonette found herself that summer in 1948 were to become a great spiritual oasis for thousands of future vacationers.

Bill asked Vonette to talk with Miss Mears. It was an unforgettable experience, Vonette recalls. "Miss Mears, of course, was one of the most vibrant personalities that you could ever meet. She really was waiting for me, and the entire staff, without my knowledge, had been praying for my conversion. Miss Mears explained that she had taught chemistry in Minneapolis and that she could understand how I was thinking. I had minored in chemistry in college and everything had to be very practical and workable to me. This was one of the reasons I had questioned Christianity.

"As she explained simply to me from God's Word how I could be sure I knew God, she used terminology very familiar to me. Her approach was that God loved me, and that if I had been the only person in all the world God would have done everything he could to reveal himself to me, that he had a plan and purpose for me that was far beyond that which I could possibly imagine. However, before I could know that plan and purpose, it was necessary for me to know God.

"Then she explained that just as a person going into a chemistry laboratory to perform an experiment follows the table of chemical valence, so is it possible for a person to enter God's laboratory and to follow his formulas of knowing him and following him. She lovingly proceeded to explain that the basic reason man does not know God is because he is sinful and separated from God. When she said man is sinful, my reaction was: 'Speak for yourself, sister; that doesn't apply to me—I've worked at this business of being a good girl.' Then, as she showed me in Romans 3:23 that 'All have sinned and fallen short of the glory of God,' and explained that sin is simply falling short of God's best or God's perfection, I suddenly realized that this was my daily experience.

"I recalled how I had kept lists of areas of my life to be improved and how desperately I worked at being more loving, considerate, helpful and neater. Miss Mears didn't have to draw a picture for me—I knew I fell short of God's best or God's perfection. She went on to show me Romans 6:23: 'For the wages (meaning payment, or salary, or results) of sin (spiritual separation from God) is death (meaning a continued spiritual separation); but the gift of God is eternal life through Jesus Christ our Lord.' It was at this point that I began to consider who Jesus Christ is.

"I had to admit that I did not really know who he is. A verse of Scripture caused me to make an about-face. In John 14:6 Jesus says, 'I am the Way, the Truth, and the Life; no man cometh unto the Father, but by me.' I realized I had tried to live a good life, had kept a high moral standard, and had been active in church. In spite of this I knew there was something missing in my life—perhaps Jesus Christ was the 'ingredient' I needed in my life formula! I turned to Miss Mears and said, 'If Jesus Christ is the Way, then how do I have him?' "

Miss Mears responded, "In Revelation 3:20 Christ says, 'Behold, I stand at the door and knock; if any man hear my voice, and open the door, I will come in to him, and sup with him, and he with me.' Receiving Christ is simply a matter of turning your life completely over to him—your will, emotions, intellect. It is as if we walk out of our lives and Jesus Christ walks in. He takes control. John 1:12 says, 'But as many as received him, to them gave he power to become the sons of God, even to them that believe on his name.' "

Vonette thought, "If what she tells me is true, I have absolutely nothing to lose and everything to gain." She bowed her head to pray.

I asked Christ to come into my heart. God became a reality in my life in an unusual way—I do not mean that a similar experience of emotional feeling has to occur when someone else receives Christ. But I do not swim; as a matter of fact I almost lost my life in a swimming course in college. I passed the course, but have not jumped off a diving board since. At the time I received Christ, the picture that came to my mind was one I shall never forget. I was standing in utter darkness on the edge of a diving board. I did not know whether or not I could swim, but I knew I had to jump—and I found out that I could swim and that God is real!"

In the following days Vonette discovered, as Miss Mears had pointed out, that walking with Christ in control is a moment-by-moment experience. God's direction in her life became a reality as she found her strong will and temper easier to control, and knew that her prayers were being heard because she saw and felt the answers. The Bible became a living Book, a guide for her everyday life.

At this time Bill came to the conclusion that God had a definite call for him to the Gospel ministry. Previously he had taken some training at Princeton Seminary, and now he went to Fuller Seminary in Pasadena, California. On December 30, 1948, Bill and Vonette were married. In her words: "Thus began the greatest adventure of my life, not only being married, but also being a Christian."

The Brights moved near the UCLA campus in 1951, to begin the ministry that would develop into Campus Crusade for Christ. "Bill had felt during his senior year at Fuller that God had given him a vision of what he was to do. He had led deputation teams to jails, road camps, churches, and so forth for a number of years, and had become concerned that no one was going to the college campus. Having been extremely active as a student in student affairs, he felt that if someone had come to him with a positive Christian message at the time he was in college he would have been interested. Yet no one had ever talked with him about Christian things, and he felt other students would be as responsive at this time in their lives as he would have been.

"Bill organized a team to go the fraternities, sororities, and the various residental groups at USC and UCLA. The students were very responsive; but we could see that to be really effective in sharing the Gospel message, we should be interdenominational and emphasize the person of Jesus Christ.

"We lived a block and a half from Miss Mears and one block from UCLA. Students would pour into our home, and it quickly became like Grand Central Station.

"That first year we organized a continuous prayer chain by dividing twenty-four hours into ninety-six fifteen-minute periods. People from all over the country were praying in fifteen-minute intervals. That year we saw about 250 students respond to the Gospel message of Christ. By the fall of 1952, we realized we needed full-time staff members. We had five young men who were joining our staff, but we had no young women to work with women students. I prayed earnestly that God might give me the opportunity to work with the students. I desired so much to work along with Bill in this ministry.

"In the early months of our marriage, as I observed Colleen Townsend and Connie Haynes and a number of the young actresses who were dedicated Christians, I had thought Bill had chosen the wrong wife because I was so spiritually immature in comparison to them. I longed to be all God wanted me to be, and to be the wife Bill needed. I learned through this experience not to desire to be used by God in the same way he uses others, or to try to imitate someone else. I learned I was to look only to Jesus and give myself to him with complete abandonment. Then he would make me the kind of person he wanted me to be."

All this time Vonette had been teaching. A new school term was just two weeks away and she was due to begin again. Then God answered her prayer in a wonderful way, through a business investment which supplied additional income, so it was no longer necessary for her to teach. Now she was free to devote her time and energies to working with girls on campus.

By the end of 1952 they needed a place where the students could congregate in large numbers. Miss Mears had been observing the growth, and in 1953 she and the Brights combined their households to meet the growing need for space.

Miss Mears bought a large home on Sunset Boulevard, and Bill and Vonette assumed the responsibility of running it and shared the living expenses.

"Many of our mutual friends thought we had all lost our minds," Vonette confides, "and they gave us three months to find out that such an arrangement would not work. But Miss Mears was mature enough to understand our immaturity and we were young enough to adjust to what needed to be done to make her happy. Actually it was a marvelous arrangement. There was much that God had to teach all of us. We lived together for almost ten years, and next to my husband Miss Mears was my closest companion. I admired and loved her so much that no matter what she said or did I trusted her judgment. I knew that she was truly led by God in her opinions and the manner in which she did her work.

"In 1954 our first child, Zachary Dale, was born and my life took on another dimension. With students coming and going at all hours, it wasn't easy to keep domestic help. At first it was a great challenge to me for I was not afraid of housework, and being a home economist I felt certain I could keep a twenty-room house running smoothly and still find time to maintain a full schedule of meetings with college girls."

At this time Vonette experienced a time of discouragement and felt the need for special spiritual counsel. But she learned that God is our best counselor, that he never tells our problems to anyone else and his counsel is more valid than any human can give.

While attending a seminar that Dr. Bob Munger was teaching, she heard him say that dissatisfaction and discouragement are not of God. He went on to say we can ask God to remove the circumstances causing us to be discouraged, and if he does not then we are to ask God to make us willing to learn what he wishes to teach us from these circumstances.

"I prayed that God would remove us from that large home. He did not, and I will never forget the morning when I finally, in tears, said, 'All right, God, if you are not going to take me out of this house, then you've got to make me be willing to learn what it is you want me to learn from this situation.' "

Shortly after that she heard a statement that George Eliot, a critic of Christianity, had made. The poet had said, "The problem with Christians is that they do not allow their celestial knowledge to affect their domestic action." Refuting this criticism became the motto of Vonette's kitchen as she began to pray that God would be glorified in whatever she had to do.

"At first it was hard—many times I stood at the kitchen sink while 250 students were in the other rooms with staff members who were not so qualified to talk with them as I thought I was. I felt that the staff members should be washing the dishes and I should be talking with the students, but then I realized that they would not receive their training by washing dishes. I began to thank God for the dishes, and it was fantastic to see what God did. He changed my attitude, and caused me to learn that it is really our attitude which determines our happiness.

"I could not change my attitude, but I could avail myself of God who could! I found the house began to go like clock-work, and I had some help who came to relieve in some of the more difficult tasks. Now I was going about with a song in my heart, realizing this was what God wanted me to do, and if this was the way in which I could please him most this was what I wanted to do. He organized that home in the most amazing manner, and I could not have been happier. Then, when I had learned the lesson he wanted me to learn, along came someone to work. By this time I wasn't so sure I wanted help because my schedule would be upset again.

"What I learned through this experience is the practicalness of being filled with the Holy Spirit. I learned that God does not want us to work for him—he wants to do his work in and through us. He doesn't want to be our helper, but he wants to do it. Knowing this has brought about the most marvelous experience of a moment-by-moment walk in fellowship with him.

"We longed for more children, but it wasn't until I was willing to say, 'Lord, I'll be happy with one little boy if you are not going to give us any more children,' that God gave us our second son, Bradley Randolph, in 1958. Our sons have taught us so very much of God's love and patience. They have taught us many spiritual lessons. I have learned how easy it is to get out of fellowship with God in the discipline of my children. I cannot help losing my temper with them, but if I ask God to take control I find my discipline is no less severe, but the way it is administered is far different.

"Bill and I have a harmonious marriage relationship. It is not that I always agree completely with my husband. In fact, I agree with Mrs. Billy Graham who says, 'If two people agree on everything, one of them is unnecessary.'

"The secret of our relationship is two-fold. First, in the beginning of our marriage we established our home with prayer, and we have practiced praying together at night before we go to bed. This has kept us in a right relationship with each other as well as with God. When there is something wrong, it's automatically confessed to God and to each other. So we go to bed in love and wake up the next morning the same way.

"The second phase is that of allowing Christ to live his life in and through us. The moment I walk out of fellowship, I need only confess to God that I am trying to live in my own strength; I am looking to self; it is ego that is in control. I ask God to take over by acknowledging I John 1:9, 'If we confess our sins, he is faithful and just to forgive us our sins, and to cleanse us from all unrighteousness.' Christ is in control of Bill's life and Christ is in control of mine, so harmony results. Christ does not war against himself. When ego is in control of one of our lives, there is disharmony, and should ego ever be in control of both our lives at the same time there would be civil war!"

In 1962 the Brights felt that Campus Crusade for Christ needed a central headquarters. Though a small conference center in Minnesota had been given to them, they had looked all over the United States for a place where they could have offices, a training center, magazine production space and shipping department. The Arrowhead Springs Hotel near San Bernardino, California, had been mentioned to them some years before, but Bill had not considered it seriously because it seemed too big a project. With every other door seemingly closed, they began to consider that Arrowhead Springs might be God's provision.

"Since the beginning of Campus Crusade for Christ," Vonette explains, "we have asked God to do everything about this work in such a miraculous way that no man would ever be able to take the credit. Thus, in a miraculous way, Arrowhead Springs Hotel with 1,800 acres surrounding it was made available to us. We established our international headquarters there, and this began another phase of my life."

Leaving Miss Mears was not easy. "We had accomplished the hurdles of adjustment and living together, and God had given us a marvelous relationship. She had been very ill during the last year we had been together, and this had drawn us closer. When we began to consider moving to Arrowhead Springs, the only part that did not seem to work smoothly was that we could not find someone to live with Miss Mears.

"This caused us great concern, but she encouraged us to continue to plan to move because she felt God had a change in store for her. The weekend of our first Lay Conference at Arrowhead, Miss Mears came to visit and she closed the meeting with prayer. She was able to see us in our new surroundings and was thrilled with what God had provided.

"Miss Mears' encouragement was a great source of inspiration for us many times, particularly until the property was paid for. One month to the day from her return from her vacation and the time she was to be with us at Arrowhead Springs, God called her to be with himself. This was a great loss to us personally, and yet the inspiration of her life is a daily experience. Her words ring in my ears at every decision, at every thought of the way in which things should be done. Of course, she had a profound impact upon my life. What God has in store for me as the result of having lived with this marvelous Christian woman, I cannot imagine. I have begun to experience in a small degree what it is to trust him for large things. She said many times in the later months of her life that if she had her life to live over, she would just simply believe God. That is the thought that I so many times practice and endeavor to pass on to others—to *believe him.*"

New opportunities for service are constantly arising for Vonette and Bill Bright and to all those who are a part of the worldwide program of Campus Crusade for Christ International.

It had long been a desire of Vonette's to connect her home economics training with her Christian experience. She is now seeing this develop in a new phase of Campus Crusade training of laymen and women. Acts 1:8 has become a reality to the Brights, "But ye shall receive power, after that the Holy Ghost is come upon you: and ye shall be witnesses unto me, both in Jerusalem, and in all Judea, and in Samaria, and unto the uttermost part of the earth."

Cinderella is a delightful story, but it is not half as wonderful as real life, Vonette Bright says. "Our lives have been a great adventure, and little do we know what God has yet in store. We simply make ourselves available to him to be used toward the fulfillment of the Great Commission within our generation. To him be all honor and glory for what has been accomplished."

Cameo sixteen

Destiny Unlimited

Plain Jane

Cameo sixteen is you, the reader, unknown to the author of this book, but known to God. You also have a story, though it may not be written and printed. And you have a God-given life to live, with some of the trials and some of the triumphs that you have read about in these stories.

Everyone chooses—somewhere in life—whom and what she will live for. Perhaps you have already chosen to live for God and have discovered that this is possible only when Jesus Christ is living in you. He is the only one whose life completely pleased God the Father—because he is God the Son. And he, in the person of the Holy Spirit, enters the life of any woman who confesses her sin to God and believes on Jesus Christ as her personal Savior. What glorious changes came into the lives of the "Cameos" when they received Jesus Christ!

If you have never received Jesus Christ, or you thought you had but your life has not changed, you may genuinely receive him now if you truly want to. One of the clearest explanations of the way to receive Christ is described by Bill Bright of Campus Crusade. He calls it "God's Four Spiritual Laws."

Law One is: *God loves you, and has a wonderful plan for your life*. This law is stated in these Bible verses: "For God so loved the world that he gave his only begotten Son, that whosoever believeth in him should not perish, but have

161

everlasting life" (John 3:16); "I (Jesus) am come that they might have life, and that they might have it more abundantly" (John 10:10b).

Law Two is: *Man is sinful and separated from God, thus he cannot know and experience God's love and plan for his life.* This is shown by Romans 3:23 and 6:23—"For all have sinned and come short of the glory of God"; "The wages of sin is death."

Law Three says: *Jesus Christ is God's only provision for man's sin; through him you can know God's love and plan for your life.* We see this in the following verses: "But God proves his love for us, in that while we were yet sinners, Christ died for us" (Romans 5:8); "Jesus saith unto him, 'I am the way, the truth, and the life; no man cometh unto the Father, but by me" (John 14:6); "For he [God the Father] hath made him [Christ the Son] to be sin for us, who knew no sin, that we might be made the righteousness of God in him" (2 Corinthians 5:21).

Law Four is: *We must receive Jesus Christ as Savior and Lord by personal invitation.* This is clear from John 1:12 and Revelation 3:20—"But as many as received him, to them gave he power to become the sons of God, even to them that believe in his name"; "Behold I [Christ] stand at the door and knock; if any man hear my voice, and open the door, I will come in."*

Jesus Christ waits at the door of every human spirit until he is either turned away or invited in. When a person is ready to turn over his life to God because he is sick of his sin and loves Christ for dying for him on the cross, then Christ comes in and new, eternal life begins.

Jesus paid the penalty for mankind's sins when he died on the cross, and he becomes the Savior of each person who trusts him. The changes in life, the thrills and victories and accomplishments—sometimes in the depths of frustrations and troubles—come as the Christian learns to surrender her own will and way to Jesus Christ. As Christ becomes more and more the Lord of the Christian's life, joy and fulfillment flood in, just as we read in the lives of the Cameos.

*The "Four Spiritual Laws" are copyrighted in this form by Campus Crusade for Christ, San Bernardino, California.

God is fashioning lovely, eternal Cameos. As one Cameo to another, may I encourage you, dear reader, to trust God to make you a precious jewel reflecting his infinite glory.